سورة الإسراء

SOORAH AL-ISRAA'
CHAPTER 17 OF THE NOBLE QURAN

RESOURCES FOR YOUR 30-DAY STUDY
OF THE COMMENTARY OF AL-IMAM AS-SA'DEE
WORKBOOK PREPARED BY: MOOSAA RICHARDSON

THIS COPY BELONGS TO:

كل الحقوق محفوظة

Copyright © 1444 (2023) by Moosaa Richardson.

All rights reserved. No part of this publication may be reproduced, distributed, or transmitted in any form or by any means, including photocopying, recording, or other electronic or mechanical methods, without the prior written permission of the copyright holder, except in the case of brief quotations embodied in critical reviews and certain other noncommercial uses permitted by copyright law.

First Print (Paperback) Edition: Rajab 1444 (February 2023)

Richardson, Moosaa. (Author)

Harding, Gibril (Proofreader)

Soorah al-Israa', Chapter 17 of the Noble Quran (Workbook) / Resources For Your 30-Day Study of the Commentary of al-Imam as-Sa'dee

ISBN: 979-8376838389

1. Nonfiction —Religion —Islam —Koran & Sacred Writings.

2. Nonfiction —Religion —Islam —General.

TABLE OF CONTENTS

PREFACE TO THE WORKBOOK	5
INTRODUCTION: ABOUT SOORAH AL-ISRAA' & THESE LESSONS	9
PERSONAL PROGRESS TRACKER	10
LESSON 1: THE NIGHT JOURNEY (AL-ISRAA' & AL-MI'RAAJ)	11
LESSON 2: FORETOLD CORRUPTION & ITS CONSEQUENCES	13
LESSON 3: THE SECOND EVENT OF FORETOLD CORRUPTION	15
LESSON 4: THE QURAN'S COMPREHENSIVE GUIDANCE	17
LESSON 5: INDIVIDUAL & PERSONAL ACCOUNTABILITY	19
LESSON 6: WORLDLY ENJOYMENT VS. REWARDS OF THE HEREAFTER	21
LESSON 7: TOWHEED & DUTIFULNESS TO PARENTS	23
LESSON 8: QURANIC GUIDELINES FOR FINANCIAL MANAGEMENT	25
LESSON 9: MORE PROHIBITIONS OF DESTRUCTIVE MAJOR SINS	27
LESSON 10: RESPONSIBILITIES IN AGREEMENTS & TRANSACTIONS	29
LESSON 11: SHUN ARROGANCE & WORSHIP ALLAH ALONE	31
LESSON 12: EXALTATIONS OF ALLAH'S MAJESTY & PERFECTION	33
LESSON 13: DISBELIEVERS DO NOT BENEFIT FROM THE QURAN	35
LESSON 14: THE FLAWED LOGIC & ARROGANCE OF DISBELIEVERS	37
LESSON 15: ALLAH'S TRUE SERVANTS HAVE THE BEST SPEECH	39
LESSON 16: THE FUTILITY OF THOSE CALLED UPON BESIDES ALLAH	41
LESSON 17: STUBBORN REJECTION OF THE MOST AMAZING SIGNS	43
LESSON 18: THE ORIGIN OF IBLEES' HATRED FOR MANKIND	45
LESSON 19: ALLAH'S UNCHALLENGED LORDSHIP OVER THE CREATION	47
LESSON 20: THE CHILDREN OF ADAM HAVE BEEN TRULY HONORED	49
LESSON 21: EVEN PROPHETS NEED GUIDANCE & STABILITY FROM ALLAH	51
LESSON 22: MESSENGERS WERE ALWAYS EXPELLED FROM THEIR LANDS	53
LESSON 23: VICTORY AFTER SINCERE PRAYERS & SUPPLICATIONS	55
LESSON 24: THE QURAN IS HEALING & MERCY FOR THE BELIEVERS	57
LESSON 25: ASKING ABOUT THE ROOH WHILE REJECTING THE QURAN	59
LESSON 26: DISBELIEVERS STUBBORNLY DEMAND THINGS THEIR WAY	61
LESSON 27: REBUKE & PUNISHMENT OF THE DISBELIEVERS	63
LESSON 28: MORE IMPORTANT LESSONS FROM PHARAOH'S STORY	65
LESSON 29: HOW TRUE BELIEVERS INTERACT WITH THE QURAN	67
LESSON 30: EXALT & PRAISE ALLAH IN YOUR PRAYERS & SUPPLICATIONS	69
A FINAL WORD	71
QUIZ I: REVIEW OF WEEK 1, LESSONS 1-7 (VERSES 1-25)	73
QUIZ 2: REVIEW OF WEEK 2, LESSONS 8-14 (VERSES 26-52)	75
QUIZ 3: REVIEW OF WEEK 3, LESSONS 15-21 (VERSES 53-75)	77
QUIZ 4: REVIEW OF WEEK 4, LESSONS 22-28 (VERSES 76-105)	79
QUIZ 5: COMPREHENSIVE FINAL EXAM (VERSES 1-111)	81
APPENDIX I: SOORAH AL-ISRAA' & A TRANSLATION OF ITS MEANINGS	85
APPENDIX II: SOORAH AL-ISRAA' (ARABIC PAGES FROM THE MUSHAF)	108

The First Muslim Mosque (Al-Masjid Al-Awwal), est. 1932, located in the heart of Pittsburgh's historic Hill District, hosts a vibrant community of local and international congregants, adhering to the tenants of Orthodox Sunni/Salafi Islam, actively condemning terrorist organizations such as ISIS, Alqaeda, and the (so-called) Muslim Brotherhood.

TWITTER: @1MMPGH

WEBSITE: WWW.FIRSTMUSLIMMOSQUE.COM

EMAIL: INFO@FIRSTMUSLIMMOSQUE.COM

بسم الله الرحمن الرحيم

PREFACE

All praise is due to Allah, the Lord, Creator, and Sustainer of all things. He is *as-Samee'* Who hears all; He is *al-Baseer* Who Sees all. His perfect and wise Decree overtakes His creation. No one deserves any worship other than Him.

"Lofty and great is His status; His Honor is openly manifest. Deities worthy of worship besides Him are inconceivable. Lost into misguidance are all those who make such claims; they transgress all bounds greatly. The greatest of all created beings surrender to His Greatness. The seven heavens and the seven earths, including all those in them, are humbled into lowly submission to His Honor.

﴿ وَٱلْأَرْضُ جَمِيعًا قَبْضَتُهُۥ يَوْمَ ٱلْقِيَٰمَةِ وَٱلسَّمَٰوَٰتُ مَطْوِيَّٰتٌۢ بِيَمِينِهِۦ ﴾

"The entire earth will be in His Grasp on the Day of Judgment, and the heavens will be rolled up in His right Hand..." [39:67]

The upper and lower levels of His Creation remain in dire need of Him, absolutely impoverished, at all times and in all situations [without Him]..."[1]

By His Mercy and Wisdom, He has sent down the Quran, the most truthful Speech, to the most truthful and noble of His creation, the final seal of all prophets and messengers, Muhammad, the true worshipful slave-servant of Allah, taken from the sacred city of Makkah to the highest point within the created realm, where even the highest-ranking and most virtuous angels could not reach.

﴿ مَا زَاغَ ٱلْبَصَرُ وَمَا طَغَىٰ ۝ لَقَدْ رَأَىٰ مِنْ ءَايَٰتِ رَبِّهِ ٱلْكُبْرَىٰٓ ۝ ﴾

"The eyesight did not deviate or transgress. He did indeed see some of the great *Aayaat* (signs) of His Lord." [53:17-18]

May Allah raise his rank and grant him, his family, companions, and followers an abundance of peace.

As for what follows: It is from the great favors of our Lord that we -once again- prepare for the blessed month of Ramadhaan, *in shaa' Allah*.

For many of us, these **"Ramadhaan Lessons"** have become an essential part of our experience, and I am humbled and honored to be part of your days and nights, asking Allah to accept from me and all of you. To briefly recap what Allah has blessed us with over the last five years:

Volume 1 of this series was our study tool for the classes in Ramadhaan 1439 (2018). Thirty lessons consisted of seven modules each, with Grammar, *Tafseer*, and *Hadeeth* modules, as well as a variety of extension activities, beginning with the verses about fasting.

---

[1] *Tayseer al-Kareem ar-Rahmaan*, p.527, in explanation of *Soorah al-Israa'*, Verse 43.

Volume 2 (1440/2019) included fifteen *Tafseer* lessons and fifteen *Hadeeth* lessons on various topics. A *fatwa* from Shaykh Ibn Baaz (may Allah have Mercy on him) was included in each lesson.

Volume 3 (1441/2020) included 30 lessons on each of the four main topics: *Tafseer, Hadeeth,* Arabic, and *Tajweed.* The 30 verses of **Soorah al-Mulk** were studied, a verse a day, for each day of the month, from **four** different books of *Tafseer*! Brief lessons in *Tajweed* and Arabic were also included.

Volume 4 (1442/2021) included another set of 120 lessons in *Tafseer, Hadeeth*, Arabic (*Sarf*, or word derivatives and conjugations), and *Tajweed,* focused on **Soorah Ibraaheem**. We cut back to reading **two** (not four) books of *Tafseer* – **al-Baghawee** and **as-Sa'dee**.

Last year's **Volume 5** (1443/2022) included two lessons a day in study of **Soorah Ghaafir**, from those same two books of *Tafseer*.

All five of the previous workbooks remain available on Amazon and at many Islamic bookstores in different parts of the world, and to Allah Alone is the praise. Furthermore, the recordings from all those activities remain easily accessible at al-Masjid al-Awwal's free public radio station:

▶ **www.Spreaker.com/user/radio1mm**

You may have noticed that we have departed from some of our established patterns this year. Our workbook is **not** called *Ramadhaan Lessons From the Noble Quran and Authentic Sunnah, Volume 6*, as you may have been expecting. There are a couple of reasons for this. Firstly, this year's lessons do not include any regular Hadeeth studies from the Sunnah. Secondly, a decision was made to end our five-year run with last year's Volume 5, so as to renew our focus on those sets of lessons and resources, and to prepare a new hardcover textbook for each of the five volumes, one for each year, over the next five years, *in shaa' Allah*. We ask Allah for success in this goal.

WHAT'S NEW WITH THIS YEAR'S LESSONS?

So this workbook and this year's Ramadhaan 1444 (2023) classes will be a study of the tremendous 17th chapter of the Quran, **Soorah al-Israa'**, also called **Soorah Banee Israa'eel**. While we have certainly down-sized the scope of the lessons and workbook this year, with only 30 Tafseer lessons in total, there is an angle to say, "Less is more!"

1. MORE FOCUS ON AL-IMAM AS-SA'DEE

Our focused study of only one book of *Tafseer* allows us to zoom in a little more than we normally would, getting more of a feel for the style and methodology of the amazing explanation of **al-Imam as-Sa'dee** (may Allah have Mercy on him).

2. BACK TO LIVE BROADCASTS

By popular demand, we return to (mostly) live sessions, broadcast right from our beloved masjid in Pittsburgh, the First Muslim Mosque, *in shaa' Allah*. The high-quality MP3 recordings of our live classes remain available for those who could not attend, to listen in whenever that is easy. *(Check out the easy visual guide on page 72.)*

3. WEEKLY QUIZZES AND A FINAL EXAM

This year's workbook introduces a new feature: weekly quizzes and a final exam. After each set of seven lessons, you will have an opportunity to review and test your understanding of that week's classes with a 10-question multiple-choice quiz, *in shaa' Allah*. Additionally, a 25-question comprehensive final exam is available. These resources, along with a complete answer key, are found on **pages 73-84** of this workbook.

4. A PERSONAL PROGRESS TRACKER

To help you manage all these resources and stay on track throughout the month, our uniquely designed **Personal Progress Tracker** provides more structure to your study. With it, you can track your daily progress and weekly quiz scores, *in shaa' Allah*. Adding in your final exam score after you review the month's lessons, you will get a total score out of 100 points. This helpful tool is found on **page 10** of this workbook.

SOME OF THE MAIN THEMES OF SOORAH AL-ISRAA'

Despite its name, *Soorah al-Israa'* does not actually provide much elaboration on the topic of the miraculous Night Journey (*al-Israa' wal-Mi'raaj*) of our Prophet (may Allah raise his rank and grant him peace), other than two brief references to it (v.1, 60), while it is full of rich meanings and guidance on other important topics.

Similar to other early Makkan chapters of the Quran, *Soorah al-Israa'* includes a heavy focus on the Hereafter (v.8-10, 13-14, 18, 51-52, 71-72, 79, 97), the nature of mankind (v.11, 53, 60, 82, 89, 100), descriptions of the believers (v.9, 19, 25, 82, 107) and disbelievers (v.10, 18, 40, 45-52, 73-76, 90-100), and warnings about Hell (v.8, 10, 18, 57, 63, 97).

Making this *soorah* especially impactful in Ramadhaan, it includes many repeated reminders about the Quran and its role in the life of a believer (v.9, 41, 45-46, 60, 78, 82, 86, 88-89, 106-107). Commands to worship Allah alone (v.2, 22-23, 39, 41, 67, 107, 110-111) are paired with mention of many of His Attributes (v.1, 17, 25, 30, 44, 61, 96), with a special focus on His Mercy (v.8, 28, 54, 57, 66, 87, 100, 110). His Qadar (divine pre-ordainment) is an oft-repeated theme as well (v.4, 5, 7, 16, 23, 58). We are reminded much in this *soorah* about our need for regular prayers (v.78-79, 107-110) and supplication (v.11, 24, 80, 108, 110-111).

Furthermore, Allah reminds us of many of His numerous and various blessings upon us (v.1-3, 6, 9, 12, 20-21, 30-31, 40, 66-67, 70, 82-83, 87). We are reminded about the nature of the devil and his strategy (v.27, 63, 61-65). We are admonished about individual accountability (v.7, 15) and guided to the traits of those who best exemplify true servitude to Him (v.1, 3, 53, 65). These are some of the commonly repeated themes we will study in this tremendous chapter, *in shaa' Allah*.

WHY NOT USE THE KHAN/HILALI TRANSLATION?

Since the translation of the meanings of the Noble Quran by Khan and Hilali is the best one available in the English language, one might be curious to know why we did not use it for *Soorah al-Israa'* in our workbook. To understand our choice, one must understand the complexities of translating the meanings of the Quran. The Quran is the miraculous and amazing Speech of Allah. Sometimes, a Verse has more than one angle of intended meaning, which requires a translator to choose one of them in how he/she will represent that in the translated expression. Some choices made by Khan/Hilali simply do not match the choices of al-Imam as-Sa'dee. Three examples of such differences in interpretation are as follows:

Verse 12: Khan/Hilali interpreted the *"hisaab"* which the people will learn as "the reckoning," which can be confusing for someone following the explanation of as-Sa'dee.

Verse 16: Khan/Hilali explained Allah's **"order"** as a legislated command to obey Him (which was violated), while as-Sa'dee explained this as a Qadar-based decree of disobedience.

Verse 73 & 76: Khan/Hilali interpreted the word *"kaadoo"* as "about to" (nearly do those things), while as-Sa'dee explained that word in both occasions as "to plot" to do those things.

HOW TO ACCESS THE RECORDINGS

Go to *www.Spreaker.com/user/radio1mm* on your computer, phone, or smart device, and then scroll down on the main page under the title, **"PODCASTS"**. Click on **"1444 (2023) Ramadhaan Lessons,"** and you will then see a list of all available class recordings. Save the page's location or create a shortcut to it, so you can return to it easily. There is an easy visual guide which demonstrates exactly how you can access these free online classes on **page 72**.

PRINT OR ELECTRONIC VERSION?

These workbooks have been prepared to accompany our courses as traditionally printed paperback workbooks, available in hardcover editions as well. They have been adapted, secondarily, as Kindle print replicas and in PDF format. This is primarily for our brothers and sisters in different parts of the world who follow the classes but cannot obtain the printed versions in their location. Others may prefer the electronic versions, as they have devices which allow note-taking. Without a device that allows easy note-taking, we highly recommend the print versions of the workbooks (paperback or hardcover).

As you most likely already know, **our workbooks have not been designed for independent self-study.** To achieve the intended benefit from these lessons, attend our free online classes daily, or listen to the recordings whenever that is easy for you, and follow along using this workbook.

May Allah reward my ever-supportive wife and family, my beloved community at the First Muslim Mosque of Pittsburgh, my respected companions, Gibril Harding and Abdul-Muhaymin ibn James, for their meticulous review and helpful suggestions, and all of those who study with us and support these efforts, wherever they may be. I ask Allah that He grant me and all of you success in attaining His Pleasure and in drawing near to Him. May He raise the rank of his Messenger, Muhammad, and grant him and his family and companions peace.

ABUL-'ABBAAS
MOOSAA RICHARDSON
Education Director
First Muslim Mosque
Pittsburgh, Pennsylvania
Email: MR@bakkah.net
Twitter: @1MMeducation

(Asking Allah to make this a blessed month for you.)

INTRODUCTION

ABOUT SOORAH AL-ISRAA' & THESE LESSONS

ABOUT THE SOORAH

1. Its names, general theme & main topics

2. Is it *Makkee* or *Madanee*? And what is the difference?

ABOUT THESE LESSONS

3. Who was as-Sa'dee?

4. About the *Tafseer* of as-Sa'dee

5. About these daily lessons

Serious students may use the following *Personal Progress Tracker* to monitor their completion of the course, as explained on page 7, in the *Preface*. Students who complete the course are encouraged to go back and review their memorization and understanding of the entire text every six months or so.

PERSONAL PROGRESS TRACKER

DAY	FOCUS OF STUDY	STUDIED	MEMORIZED	SCORE
1	SOORAH AL-ISRAA' VERSE 1	☐ 0.5	☐ 0.5	___ / 1
2	SOORAH AL-ISRAA' VERSES 2-5	☐ 0.5	☐ 0.5	___ / 1
3	SOORAH AL-ISRAA' VERSES 6-8	☐ 0.5	☐ 0.5	___ / 1
4	SOORAH AL-ISRAA' VERSES 9-12	☐ 0.5	☐ 0.5	___ / 1
5	SOORAH AL-ISRAA' VERSES 13-17	☐ 0.5	☐ 0.5	___ / 1
6	SOORAH AL-ISRAA' VERSES 18-22	☐ 0.5	☐ 0.5	___ / 1
7	SOORAH AL-ISRAA' VERSES 23-25	☐ 0.5	☐ 0.5	___ / 1
●	QUIZ 1: LESSONS 1-7 (VERSES 1-25) & MEMORIZATION CHECK			___ / 10
8	SOORAH AL-ISRAA' VERSES 26-30	☐ 0.5	☐ 0.5	___ / 1
9	SOORAH AL-ISRAA' VERSES 31-33	☐ 0.5	☐ 0.5	___ / 1
10	SOORAH AL-ISRAA' VERSES 34-36	☐ 0.5	☐ 0.5	___ / 1
11	SOORAH AL-ISRAA' VERSES 37-40	☐ 0.5	☐ 0.5	___ / 1
12	SOORAH AL-ISRAA' VERSES 41-44	☐ 0.5	☐ 0.5	___ / 1
13	SOORAH AL-ISRAA' VERSES 45-48	☐ 0.5	☐ 0.5	___ / 1
14	SOORAH AL-ISRAA' VERSES 49-52	☐ 0.5	☐ 0.5	___ / 1
●	QUIZ 2: LESSONS 8-14 (VERSES 26-52) & MEMORIZATION CHECK			___ / 10
15	SOORAH AL-ISRAA' VERSES 53-55	☐ 0.5	☐ 0.5	___ / 1
16	SOORAH AL-ISRAA' VERSES 56-58	☐ 0.5	☐ 0.5	___ / 1
17	SOORAH AL-ISRAA' VERSES 59-60	☐ 0.5	☐ 0.5	___ / 1
18	SOORAH AL-ISRAA' VERSES 61-65	☐ 0.5	☐ 0.5	___ / 1
19	SOORAH AL-ISRAA' VERSES 66-69	☐ 0.5	☐ 0.5	___ / 1
20	SOORAH AL-ISRAA' VERSES 70-72	☐ 0.5	☐ 0.5	___ / 1
21	SOORAH AL-ISRAA' VERSES 73-75	☐ 0.5	☐ 0.5	___ / 1
●	QUIZ 3: LESSONS 15-22 (VERSES 53-75) & MEMORIZATION CHECK			___ / 10
22	SOORAH AL-ISRAA' VERSES 76-77	☐ 0.5	☐ 0.5	___ / 1
23	SOORAH AL-ISRAA' VERSES 78-81	☐ 0.5	☐ 0.5	___ / 1
24	SOORAH AL-ISRAA' VERSES 82-84	☐ 0.5	☐ 0.5	___ / 1
25	SOORAH AL-ISRAA' VERSES 85-88	☐ 0.5	☐ 0.5	___ / 1
26	SOORAH AL-ISRAA' VERSES 89-96	☐ 0.5	☐ 0.5	___ / 1
27	SOORAH AL-ISRAA' VERSES 97-100	☐ 0.5	☐ 0.5	___ / 1
28	SOORAH AL-ISRAA' VERSES 101-105	☐ 0.5	☐ 0.5	___ / 1
●	QUIZ 4: LESSONS 22-28 (VERSES 76-105) & MEMORIZATION CHECK			___ / 10
29	SOORAH AL-ISRAA' VERSES 106-109	☐ 0.5	☐ 0.5	___ / 1
30	SOORAH AL-ISRAA' VERSES 110-111	☐ 0.5	☐ 0.5	___ / 1
●	QUIZ 5: COMPREHENSIVE FINAL EXAM (VERSES 1-111)			___ / 25
●	COMPREHENSIVE MEMORIZATION CHECK (VERSES 1-111)			___ / 5

TOTAL = ___ %

LESSON 1

THE NIGHT JOURNEY (AL-ISRAA' & AL-MI'RAAJ)

TODAY'S VERSE

قال تعالى: بِسْمِ اللَّهِ الرَّحْمَٰنِ الرَّحِيمِ

﴿سُبْحَانَ الَّذِي أَسْرَىٰ بِعَبْدِهِ لَيْلًا مِّنَ الْمَسْجِدِ الْحَرَامِ إِلَى الْمَسْجِدِ الْأَقْصَى الَّذِي بَارَكْنَا حَوْلَهُ لِنُرِيَهُ مِنْ آيَاتِنَا ۚ إِنَّهُ هُوَ السَّمِيعُ الْبَصِيرُ ۝﴾

In the Name of Allah, the Most Gracious, the Ever Merciful.

1. Exalted is He (Allah) Who took His slave for a journey by night from the sacred *masjid* (in Makkah) to the farthest *masjid* (in Jerusalem), which We had blessed all its surrounding areas, in order that We might show him some of Our *Aayaat* (proofs, evidences, signs, etc.). Verily, it is He (Allah) [Alone] Who is the All-Hearing, the All-Seeing.

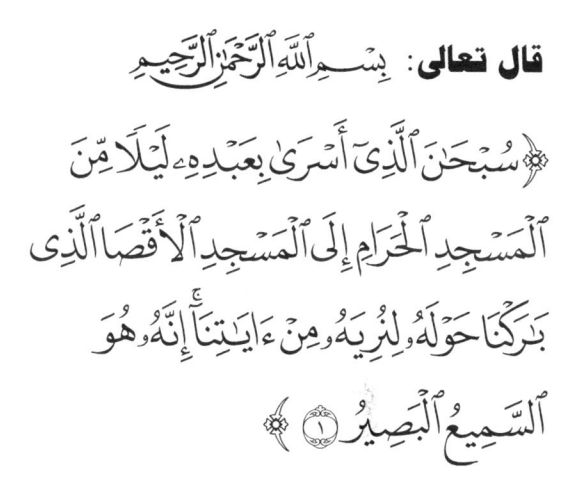

TAFSEER (EXPLANATION) OF THE VERSE

As your teacher reads the *Tafseer* of al-Imam as-Sa'dee (may Allah have Mercy on him), follow along carefully and take notes on the following points:

1. Another name for this *soorah* is:

2. This *soorah* is *Makkiyyah* / *Madaniyyah*. (Circle one.)

3. Summarize some differences between *Makkiyyah* and *Madaniyyah* Verses:

MAKKIYYAH	MADANIYYAH

4. Allah exalts Himself by mentioning:

   In general:

   Specifically:

5. Who is **"His *'abd*"** [slave/servant/worshipper]?

6. What is **al-Masjid al-Haraam** and what special status does it hold?

11

7. What is **al-Masjid al-Aqsaa** and what special status does it hold?

8. How long did this night journey take?

9. Four benefits of what he was shown that night:

10. How does this event indicate Allah's special care of His **'abd**?

    A.

    B.

11. What part of the night specifically did this journey take place?

12. From where did he actually depart?

    A. Apparent:

    B. More accurate:

13. A deduction based on that second position (12-B):

14. Was this night journey a spiritual journey of the soul?

15. A summary of the details of the night journey from Hadeeth narrations:

16. Why was he referred to here as an **'abd** (slave/servant/messenger)?

17. Other occasions when he was called an **'abd**:

    A.

    B.

18. Ways **al-Masjid al-Aqsaa** and its surrounding areas are blessed:

    A.

    B.

    C.

    D.

LESSON 2

FORETOLD CORRUPTION & ITS CONSEQUENCES

TODAY'S VERSES

قال تعالى:

2. We had given Moosaa (Moses) the Book and made it guidance for the Children of Israel (saying): "Do not take other than Me as a protecting ally.

3. O descendants of those whom We carried [in the ship] along with Nooh (Noah)! Verily, he was a grateful slave."

4. We decreed for the Children of Israel in the Book, that you would in fact cause corruption on earth twice, and that you would actually become tyrants and extremely arrogant!

5. So when the set time came for the first of the two [decrees], We sent against you slaves of Ours, possessors of tremendous strength and might. They entered the very innermost parts of your homes; that was a promised event, fully enacted.

﴿ وَءَاتَيْنَا مُوسَى ٱلْكِتَٰبَ وَجَعَلْنَٰهُ هُدًى لِّبَنِىٓ إِسْرَٰٓءِيلَ أَلَّا تَتَّخِذُوا۟ مِن دُونِى وَكِيلًا ۝ ذُرِّيَّةَ مَنْ حَمَلْنَا مَعَ نُوحٍ إِنَّهُۥ كَانَ عَبْدًا شَكُورًا ۝ وَقَضَيْنَآ إِلَىٰ بَنِىٓ إِسْرَٰٓءِيلَ فِى ٱلْكِتَٰبِ لَتُفْسِدُنَّ فِى ٱلْأَرْضِ مَرَّتَيْنِ وَلَتَعْلُنَّ عُلُوًّا كَبِيرًا ۝ فَإِذَا جَآءَ وَعْدُ أُولَىٰهُمَا بَعَثْنَا عَلَيْكُمْ عِبَادًا لَّنَآ أُو۟لِى بَأْسٍ شَدِيدٍ فَجَاسُوا۟ خِلَٰلَ ٱلدِّيَارِ وَكَانَ وَعْدًا مَّفْعُولًا ۝ ﴾

TAFSEER (EXPLANATION) OF THE VERSES

As your teacher reads the *Tafseer* of al-Imam as-Sa'dee (may Allah have Mercy on him), follow along carefully and take notes on the following points:

1. Allah mentions these two prophets together often, due to:

    A.

    B.

    C.

    D.

2. The Book given to Moosaa:

3. The Children of Israel were guided:

    A. From:

    B. To:

13

4. Meanings of *"Do not take other than Me as a protecting ally"*

    A.

    B.

    C.

    D.

5. Addressing them as *"Descendants of Nooh"*

6. Nooh is praised for his patience, indicating:

    A.

    B.

    C.

7. Allah decreed their corruption to happen.

8. The wisdom in mentioning the previous corruption and its consequences:

9. *"So when the set time came for the first of the two..."*

10. Allah's Decree to unleash the consequence

11. The description of those who overpowered them

12. What they did to them

13. *"A promised event, fully enacted"*

14. Who exactly were they?

15. Why were they sent?

LESSON 3

THE SECOND EVENT OF FORETOLD CORRUPTION

TODAY'S VERSES

قال تعالى:

6. After that, We granted you a return of victory against them. We provided you with wealth and children, and We made you more in number than them.

7. If you did things well, you did them well for your own souls. If you did evil, it was only against them (i.e. your souls). When the final (second) appointed time came to pass, it was to make your faces sorrowful, and for them (your enemies) to enter the *masjid* (of Jerusalem) as they had entered it before, and to destroy with utter destruction all places they gained authority over.

8. Perhaps your Lord may have Mercy on you, but if you return [to disobedience], We shall return [to punishing you]. And We made Hell to be a prison for the disbelievers.

﴿ثُمَّ رَدَدْنَا لَكُمُ ٱلْكَرَّةَ عَلَيْهِمْ وَأَمْدَدْنَكُم بِأَمْوَٰلٍ وَبَنِينَ وَجَعَلْنَكُمْ أَكْثَرَ نَفِيرًا ۝ إِنْ أَحْسَنتُمْ أَحْسَنتُمْ لِأَنفُسِكُمْ وَإِنْ أَسَأْتُمْ فَلَهَا فَإِذَا جَآءَ وَعْدُ ٱلْءَاخِرَةِ لِيَسُوءُوا۟ وُجُوهَكُمْ وَلِيَدْخُلُوا۟ ٱلْمَسْجِدَ كَمَا دَخَلُوهُ أَوَّلَ مَرَّةٍ وَلِيُتَبِّرُوا۟ مَا عَلَوْا۟ تَتْبِيرًا ۝ عَسَىٰ رَبُّكُمْ أَن يَرْحَمَكُمْ وَإِنْ عُدتُّمْ عُدْنَا وَجَعَلْنَا جَهَنَّمَ لِلْكَٰفِرِينَ حَصِيرًا ۝﴾

TAFSEER (EXPLANATION) OF THE VERSES

As your teacher reads the *Tafseer* of al-Imam as-Sa'dee (may Allah have Mercy on him), follow along carefully and take notes on the following points:

1. A return of victory against them

2. An increase of wealth and offspring

3. The reason for these blessings:

4. Good deeds benefit a person's own soul.

5. Evil deeds only harm a person's own soul.

    An example already mentioned:

6. The second set appointment

7. How were their faces made sorrowful?

15

8. Which *masjid* is being referred to in Verse #7?

9. What did they destroy?

10. **"Perhaps your Lord may have Mercy on you..."**

11. The threat of another punishment

12. And, YES, it took place! How and when?

13. But the punishment of the Hereafter is more serious.

14. The lesson in all of this for our *Ummah*

15. Reflections about the current situation of the Muslims:

    A. The root causes of harms we face:

    B. The solution and the way out:

LESSON 4

THE QURAN'S COMPREHENSIVE GUIDANCE

قال تعالى:

TODAY'S VERSES

9. Verily, this Quran guides to what is upright and gives glad tidings to the believers who work deeds of righteousness, that they shall have a great reward.

10. And [it warns that] those who do not believe in the Hereafter, for them We have prepared a painful torment.

11. Mankind supplicates for evil similar to how he supplicates for good; mankind is ever so hasty.

12. And We have made the night and the day to be two signs. We then wiped away [the light from] the sign of night, while We made the sign of day illuminating, so that you could seek bounty from your Lord, and so that you could know the number of years and [other] calculated matters. And We have explained everything in detail, with full explanation.

﴿إِنَّ هَٰذَا ٱلْقُرْءَانَ يَهْدِى لِلَّتِى هِىَ أَقْوَمُ وَيُبَشِّرُ ٱلْمُؤْمِنِينَ ٱلَّذِينَ يَعْمَلُونَ ٱلصَّٰلِحَٰتِ أَنَّ لَهُمْ أَجْرًا كَبِيرًا ۝ وَأَنَّ ٱلَّذِينَ لَا يُؤْمِنُونَ بِٱلْءَاخِرَةِ أَعْتَدْنَا لَهُمْ عَذَابًا أَلِيمًا ۝ وَيَدْعُ ٱلْإِنسَٰنُ بِٱلشَّرِّ دُعَآءَهُۥ بِٱلْخَيْرِ ۖ وَكَانَ ٱلْإِنسَٰنُ عَجُولًا ۝ وَجَعَلْنَا ٱلَّيْلَ وَٱلنَّهَارَ ءَايَتَيْنِ ۖ فَمَحَوْنَآ ءَايَةَ ٱلَّيْلِ وَجَعَلْنَا ءَايَةَ ٱلنَّهَارِ مُبْصِرَةً لِّتَبْتَغُوا۟ فَضْلًا مِّن رَّبِّكُمْ وَلِتَعْلَمُوا۟ عَدَدَ ٱلسِّنِينَ وَٱلْحِسَابَ ۚ وَكُلَّ شَىْءٍ فَصَّلْنَٰهُ تَفْصِيلًا ۝﴾

TAFSEER (EXPLANATION) OF THE VERSES

As your teacher reads the *Tafseer* of al-Imam as-Sa'dee (may Allah have Mercy on him), follow along carefully and take notes on the following points:

1. The Quran guides to all that is upright.

2. The amazing results of following the Quran's guidance:

3. Deeds of righteousness

4. A great reward

17

5. The guidance of the Quran includes:

A.	➡ C.
B.	➡ D.

6. Mankind's ignorance leads him into self-destruction!

7. The Mercy and Kindness of Allah

    (10:11)

8. What do the signs of the night and day indicate?

    A.

    B.

    C.

9. Allah *"wiped away"* the sign of the night.

10. Which favors do people seek from Allah in the daytime?

11. Knowing how to track and count days and time

12. Every matter has been clarified.

    (6:38)

LESSON 5

INDIVIDUAL & PERSONAL ACCOUNTABILITY

قال تعالى:

TODAY'S VERSES

13. For every person, We have fastened his deeds to his neck, and on the Day of Judgment, We bring forth unto him a book which he finds wide open.

14. "Read your book. You yourself are sufficient as a reckoner against you on this Day."

15. Whoever followed guidance, it is only for the benefit of his own soul. Whoever went astray, he only goes astray at his own expense. No one shall bear the burden of another, and We never punish [anyone] until We first send a messenger.

16. Whenever We want to destroy a village, We first decree that the extravagant ones among them shall disobey therein, thus the verdict [of punishment] is justified against it (the village). Then We destroy it with complete destruction.

17. And how many previous generations did We destroy after Nooh (Noah)! Sufficient is your Lord as One who is All-Knowing and All-Seeing, regarding the sins of His slaves.

﴿ وَكُلَّ إِنسَٰنٍ أَلْزَمْنَٰهُ طَٰٓئِرَهُۥ فِى عُنُقِهِۦ وَنُخْرِجُ لَهُۥ يَوْمَ ٱلْقِيَٰمَةِ كِتَٰبًا يَلْقَىٰهُ مَنشُورًا ۝ ٱقْرَأْ كِتَٰبَكَ كَفَىٰ بِنَفْسِكَ ٱلْيَوْمَ عَلَيْكَ حَسِيبًا ۝ مَّنِ ٱهْتَدَىٰ فَإِنَّمَا يَهْتَدِى لِنَفْسِهِۦ وَمَن ضَلَّ فَإِنَّمَا يَضِلُّ عَلَيْهَا وَلَا تَزِرُ وَازِرَةٌ وِزْرَ أُخْرَىٰ وَمَا كُنَّا مُعَذِّبِينَ حَتَّىٰ نَبْعَثَ رَسُولًا ۝ وَإِذَآ أَرَدْنَآ أَن نُّهْلِكَ قَرْيَةً أَمَرْنَا مُتْرَفِيهَا فَفَسَقُوا۟ فِيهَا فَحَقَّ عَلَيْهَا ٱلْقَوْلُ فَدَمَّرْنَٰهَا تَدْمِيرًا ۝ وَكَمْ أَهْلَكْنَا مِنَ ٱلْقُرُونِ مِنۢ بَعْدِ نُوحٍ وَكَفَىٰ بِرَبِّكَ بِذُنُوبِ عِبَادِهِۦ خَبِيرًۢا بَصِيرًا ۝ ﴾

TAFSEER (EXPLANATION) OF THE VERSES

As your teacher reads the *Tafseer* of al-Imam as-Sa'dee (may Allah have Mercy on him), follow along carefully and take notes on the following points:

1. The complete and perfect Justice of Allah

2. What is mankind's *"taa'ir"* (طائر)?

3. What is contained in this book?

4. The justice of taking your own soul to account on that Day

5. Personal & individual accountability

19

6. Perfect justice includes that no one is punished without proof established.

7. A deduction based on contrast

8. Two types of people who have an excuse, based on this Verse:

    A.

    B.

9. The process of destroying a place

10. *"Thus the verdict is justified..."*

11. Nations of the past were actually destroyed like this.

    Examples:

12. *"Sufficient is your Lord as One who is All-Knowing and All-Seeing..."*

    A.

    B.

LESSON 6

WORLDLY ENJOYMENT VS. REWARDS OF THE HEREAFTER

TODAY'S VERSES

قال تعالى:

18. Whoever wishes for what is quick and temporary (i.e. the enjoyment of this worldly life), We bring that forth quickly for him, whatever We want of it for him. Yet, afterwards, We have prepared *Jahannam* for him, to enter it in disgrace and humiliation.

19. Yet whoever desires the Hereafter and strives for it, with the effort appropriate for it, while being a believer, such are the ones whose striving shall be appreciated.

20. To all, these and those alike, We extend for them from the bounties of your Lord, and the bounties of your Lord are never forbidden.

21. Consider how We favor some of them over others [in this worldly life], while the Hereafter is indeed a place of greater degrees [of reward] and even more favoring [of some over others].

22. Do not set up, along with Allah, any other deity, lest you end up humiliated and forsaken [in Hell].

TAFSEER (EXPLANATION) OF THE VERSES

As your teacher reads the *Tafseer* of al-Imam as-Sa'dee (may Allah have Mercy on him), follow along carefully and take notes on the following points:

1. Whoever prefers worldly enjoyment

2. The situation of people in Hell:

    A. Disgrace

    B. Humiliation [of being abandoned]

3. The meaning of desiring the Hereafter

4. What efforts are appropriate for rewards in the Hereafter?

5. **"While being a believer..."** (in what?)

6. Their striving shall be **"mashkoor"** (مشكور)

7. Worldly provisions are still guaranteed, even when one focuses on the Hereafter.

8. No one can restrict Allah's provisions.

9. Different ways some people are preferred over others in this worldly life:

10. Worldly joys vs. enjoyment in the Hereafter

11. Comparing the consequences in the Hereafter

12. The prohibition of *shirk*

13. The consequences of *shirk*

    A.

    B.

14. A deduction based on contrast

LESSON 7

TOWHEED & DUTIFULNESS TO ONE'S PARENTS

قال تعالى:

TODAY'S VERSES

23. Your Lord has decreed that you shall not worship anyone other than Him, and that you must be dutiful to parents. If one or both of them reach old age in your life, do not say to them, *"Uff,"* (the slightest show of disrespect), nor rebuke them. Instead, only speak to them with a kind word.

24. And lower unto them the wing of humility, out of mercy, and say: "My Lord! Have Mercy on them, as they took care of me when I was young."

25. Your Lord knows best about what is within your souls. If you are righteous, then He is indeed Forgiving to those who continually and dutifully repent [to Him].

﴿۞ وَقَضَىٰ رَبُّكَ أَلَّا تَعْبُدُوٓا۟ إِلَّآ إِيَّاهُ وَبِٱلْوَٰلِدَيْنِ إِحْسَٰنًا إِمَّا يَبْلُغَنَّ عِندَكَ ٱلْكِبَرَ أَحَدُهُمَآ أَوْ كِلَاهُمَا فَلَا تَقُل لَّهُمَآ أُفٍّ وَلَا تَنْهَرْهُمَا وَقُل لَّهُمَا قَوْلًا كَرِيمًا ۝ وَٱخْفِضْ لَهُمَا جَنَاحَ ٱلذُّلِّ مِنَ ٱلرَّحْمَةِ وَقُل رَّبِّ ٱرْحَمْهُمَا كَمَا رَبَّيَانِى صَغِيرًا ۝ رَّبُّكُمْ أَعْلَمُ بِمَا فِى نُفُوسِكُمْ إِن تَكُونُوا۟ صَٰلِحِينَ فَإِنَّهُۥ كَانَ لِلْأَوَّٰبِينَ غَفُورًا ۝ ﴾

TAFSEER (EXPLANATION) OF THE VERSES

As your teacher reads the *Tafseer* of al-Imam as-Sa'dee (may Allah have Mercy on him), follow along carefully and take notes on the following points:

1. After forbidding *shirk* in Verse 22, Allah orders:

2. Which type of "*qadhaa*" (قضاء) is this?

    (Compare to Verses 4)

    (Compare to Verse 16)

3. Who should not be worshipped?

4. Why must only Allah be worshipped?

1.	4.
2.	5.
3.	6.

23

5. The great status of dutifulness to parents

6. What is the *"ihsaan"* (إحسان) which is due to them?

7. Why do parents deserve kind treatment?

8. Old age and the needs of the elderly

9. The intended meaning of *"uff"*

10. The prohibition of rebuking parents

11. **"Only speak to them with a kind word."**

12. The intention needed in one's humility with his parents

13. Supplicating for Mercy for them

14. A deduction about the intensity of the supplications

15. A deduction about teachers and other caretakers

16. **"Your Lord knows best about what is within your souls..."**

17. What it means to be righteous

    A.

    B.

18. The meaning of *"awwaaboon"* (أوابون)

19. What kind of people does Allah forgive most?

LESSON 8

QURANIC GUIDELINES FOR FINANCIAL MANAGEMENT

TODAY'S VERSES

قال تعالى:

26. And give the close relative his right, and to the poor man and the traveler as well, but do not overspend wastefully.

27. Verily, spendthrifts are the brothers of the devils, and the devil is ever ungrateful to his Lord.

28. If you turn away from them [for now], anticipating Mercy from your Lord which you hope for [to give to them later], then speak to them a gentle word.

29. Do not let your hand be tied up to your neck [in miserliness], nor stretch it forth to its utmost reach [wastefully], lest you end up blameworthy and impoverished.

30. Truly, your Lord grants abundant provisions to whomever He wills and limits that [for others]. Verily, regarding His slaves, He is All-Knowing and All-Seeing.

﴿وَءَاتِ ذَا ٱلْقُرْبَىٰ حَقَّهُۥ وَٱلْمِسْكِينَ وَٱبْنَ ٱلسَّبِيلِ وَلَا تُبَذِّرْ تَبْذِيرًا ۝ إِنَّ ٱلْمُبَذِّرِينَ كَانُوٓا۟ إِخْوَٰنَ ٱلشَّيَـٰطِينِ ۖ وَكَانَ ٱلشَّيْطَـٰنُ لِرَبِّهِۦ كَفُورًا ۝ وَإِمَّا تُعْرِضَنَّ عَنْهُمُ ٱبْتِغَآءَ رَحْمَةٍ مِّن رَّبِّكَ تَرْجُوهَا فَقُل لَّهُمْ قَوْلًا مَّيْسُورًا ۝ وَلَا تَجْعَلْ يَدَكَ مَغْلُولَةً إِلَىٰ عُنُقِكَ وَلَا تَبْسُطْهَا كُلَّ ٱلْبَسْطِ فَتَقْعُدَ مَلُومًا مَّحْسُورًا ۝ إِنَّ رَبَّكَ يَبْسُطُ ٱلرِّزْقَ لِمَن يَشَآءُ وَيَقْدِرُ ۚ إِنَّهُۥ كَانَ بِعِبَادِهِۦ خَبِيرًۢا بَصِيرًا ۝﴾

TAFSEER (EXPLANATION) OF THE VERSES

As your teacher reads the *Tafseer* of al-Imam as-Sa'dee (may Allah have Mercy on him), follow along carefully and take notes on the following points:

1. Giving the relative his right

2. Giving the poor man his right

3. The traveler, *"ibn as-sabeel"* (ابن السبيل)

4. The balance needed when taking care of others

5. The brothers of the devil

6. When the devil is disobeyed, does he give up in defeat?

25

7. Allah loves when His slaves take the middle course.

    (25:67)

8. One's hand tied up to one's neck?

9. A hand fully outstretched

10. The results of wasting wealth:

    A.

    B.

11. Guidance for each of two scenarios:

    A.

    B.

12. How to express your inability to help financially

13. The hoped result

14. Reflection: Allah's Merciful care and Kindness

    A. Hoping for provisions is worship

    B. Ambition when incapable is rewardable

15. Reflection: Doing what you can & hoping to do what you cannot

    Hopefully, the result will be:

16. Reflection: The reason for different levels of provisions

17. *"Verily, regarding His slaves, He is All-Knowing and All-Seeing"*

LESSON 9

MORE PROHIBITIONS OF DESTRUCTIVE MAJOR SINS

TODAY'S VERSES

قال تعالى:

31. Do not kill not your children in fear of poverty. We provide for them and for you. Surely, killing them is a great sin.

32. And do not come anywhere close to unlawful sexual intercourse. Verily, that is a sinful obscenity, and what an evil path it is!

33. Also, do not take any life which Allah has forbidden, except by legitimate right. Whoever is oppressively killed, We have certainly granted his heir authority [to request the death penalty or demand blood money through Islamic courts]. Yet he must not transgress limits in [seeking] the death penalty. Verily, he is one who is aided [by Allah and through His Legislation].

﴿وَلَا تَقْتُلُوٓا۟ أَوْلَٰدَكُمْ خَشْيَةَ إِمْلَٰقٍ ۖ نَّحْنُ نَرْزُقُهُمْ وَإِيَّاكُمْ ۚ إِنَّ قَتْلَهُمْ كَانَ خِطْـًٔا كَبِيرًا ۝ وَلَا تَقْرَبُوا۟ ٱلزِّنَىٰٓ ۖ إِنَّهُۥ كَانَ فَٰحِشَةً وَسَآءَ سَبِيلًا ۝ وَلَا تَقْتُلُوا۟ ٱلنَّفْسَ ٱلَّتِى حَرَّمَ ٱللَّهُ إِلَّا بِٱلْحَقِّ ۗ وَمَن قُتِلَ مَظْلُومًا فَقَدْ جَعَلْنَا لِوَلِيِّهِۦ سُلْطَٰنًا فَلَا يُسْرِف فِّى ٱلْقَتْلِ ۖ إِنَّهُۥ كَانَ مَنصُورًا ۝﴾

TAFSEER (EXPLANATION) OF THE VERSES

As your teacher reads the *Tafseer* of al-Imam as-Sa'dee (may Allah have Mercy on him), follow along carefully and take notes on the following points:

1. Allah is Merciful to His slaves

    A.

    B.

2. Why killing children is such a heinous crime

    A.

    B.

    C.

3. The prohibition of even **"approaching"** zinaa

    How inclusive & far-reaching is this?

    (Hadeeth)

27

4. Especially in an issue like this

5. *Zinaa* is a **"faahishah"** (فاحشة)

6. What makes *zinaa* so repugnant?

1.	4.
2.	5.
3.	6.

7. **"And what an evil path it is!"**

8. How inclusive is the prohibition of taking **"any life which Allah has forbidden"**?

9. When is it permissible to take a life in Islamic Law?

10. Who exactly is the **"heir"** of the victim?

11. What kind of authority does he have?

    A.

    B.

12. Forms of forbidden transgression in seeking the death penalty

13. The significance of the position of the heir

14. Special support and assistance

LESSON 10

RESPONSIBILITIES IN AGREEMENTS & TRANSACTIONS

قال تعالى:

TODAY'S VERSES

34. And do not come anywhere near the orphan's property, except in ways that are best (i.e. good investments), until he attains his age of full strength. And fulfil (every) covenant; verily, the covenants will be asked about.

35. Give full portions when you measure [your goods], and weigh [them] with fair, precise balance. That is better and finer in consequence.

36. And do not follow after what you have no knowledge of. Verily, the hearing, the sight, and the heart, all of that will be asked about.

﴿وَلَا تَقْرَبُوا مَالَ الْيَتِيمِ إِلَّا بِالَّتِي هِيَ أَحْسَنُ حَتَّىٰ يَبْلُغَ أَشُدَّهُ ۚ وَأَوْفُوا بِالْعَهْدِ ۖ إِنَّ الْعَهْدَ كَانَ مَسْئُولًا ۝ وَأَوْفُوا الْكَيْلَ إِذَا كِلْتُمْ وَزِنُوا بِالْقِسْطَاسِ الْمُسْتَقِيمِ ۚ ذَٰلِكَ خَيْرٌ وَأَحْسَنُ تَأْوِيلًا ۝ وَلَا تَقْفُ مَا لَيْسَ لَكَ بِهِ عِلْمٌ ۚ إِنَّ السَّمْعَ وَالْبَصَرَ وَالْفُؤَادَ كُلُّ أُولَٰئِكَ كَانَ عَنْهُ مَسْئُولًا ۝﴾

TAFSEER (EXPLANATION) OF THE VERSES

As your teacher reads the *Tafseer* of al-Imam as-Sa'dee (may Allah have Mercy on him), follow along carefully and take notes on the following points:

1. More proof of Allah's Mercy & Kindness

2. Who can be classified as an orphan?

3. Caretakers of orphans must uphold these four responsibilities:

4. Guidelines observed when managing an orphan's estate:

   A.

   B.

   C.

5. What exactly is the orphan's **"age of full strength"**?

29

6. What changes legally at this point, when he reaches this age?

    A.

    B.

    C.

    (4:6)

7. The command to fulfill contracts & covenants

    A.

    B.

8. Contracts & covenants will be asked about:

A.	➡ C.
B.	➡ D.

9. Quranic guidance for merchants in the marketplace

10. What is understood from this guidance:

    A. Prohibitions to avoid:

    B. Obligations to fulfill:

11. The good results of obedience to Allah in the marketplace:

    A.

    B.

12. A deduction based on the opposite meaning:

13. Preparation for being questioned, through the following steps:

    A.

    B.

    C.

LESSON 11

SHUN ARROGANCE & WORSHIP ALLAH ALONE

TODAY'S VERSES

قال تعالى:

37. And do not walk about in the land arrogantly. Verily, you cannot crack the earth, nor could you reach a stature like the mountains in height.

38. All the bad aspects of these matters are hated by your Lord.

39. That is from the wisdom which your Lord has revealed to you. And do not set up any other deity in your worship of Allah, lest you be cast down into *Jahannam*, blameworthy and rejected.

40. Has then your Lord favored you [by providing you] with sons, while He takes Angels for Himself, as female offspring? Verily, you utter such a terrible claim, indeed.

﴿وَلَا تَمْشِ فِي ٱلْأَرْضِ مَرَحًا إِنَّكَ لَن تَخْرِقَ ٱلْأَرْضَ وَلَن تَبْلُغَ ٱلْجِبَالَ طُولًا ۝ كُلُّ ذَٰلِكَ كَانَ سَيِّئُهُۥ عِندَ رَبِّكَ مَكْرُوهًا ۝ ذَٰلِكَ مِمَّآ أَوْحَىٰٓ إِلَيْكَ رَبُّكَ مِنَ ٱلْحِكْمَةِ ۗ وَلَا تَجْعَلْ مَعَ ٱللَّهِ إِلَٰهًا ءَاخَرَ فَتُلْقَىٰ فِي جَهَنَّمَ مَلُومًا مَّدْحُورًا ۝ أَفَأَصْفَىٰكُمْ رَبُّكُم بِٱلْبَنِينَ وَٱتَّخَذَ مِنَ ٱلْمَلَٰٓئِكَةِ إِنَٰثًا ۚ إِنَّكُمْ لَتَقُولُونَ قَوْلًا عَظِيمًا ۝﴾

TAFSEER (EXPLANATION) OF THE VERSES

As your teacher reads the *Tafseer* of al-Imam as-Sa'dee (may Allah have Mercy on him), follow along carefully and take notes on the following points:

1. The prohibition of walking about in arrogance

2. You will not attain status by arrogance, but instead what will happen?

    A.

    B.

    C.

3. **"All the bad aspects of these matters..."** (*Let's summarize these things.*)

31

4. The real **harms** of these matters:

5. The two basic types of **wisdom** (found in these matters):

    A.

    B.

6. How these matters are from the best kinds of wisdom

7. The great blessing of wisdom

    (2:269)

8. Concluding this series of points with a re-emphasis of the first matter

9. Being cast into Hell for this violation is for eternity.

    (5:72)

10. *"Blameworthy and rejected..."*

11. A firm rebuke against those who ascribe daughters to Allah

12. Male offspring for you, but females for Him?!

13. How terrible and audacious this claim is:

    A.

    B.

LESSON 12

EXALTATIONS OF ALLAH'S MAJESTY & PERFECTION

TODAY'S VERSES

قال تعالى:

41. And surely, We have provided [many rulings and lessons] in this Quran, in order for them to take heed, yet it only increases them in aversion [to the Truth].

42. Say: "Had there been other deities [worthy of worship] along with Him as they claim, they would certainly have sought nearness to the Owner of the Throne.

43. Exalted and Lofty He is, far above what they claim!"

44. The seven heavens and the earth and all that is within them exalt Him. There is not a thing which does not glorify Him in praise, yet you do not comprehend their exaltations. Truly, He is Ever Forbearing, Oft-Forgiving.

﴿وَلَقَدْ صَرَّفْنَا فِي هَٰذَا ٱلْقُرْءَانِ لِيَذَّكَّرُوا۟ وَمَا يَزِيدُهُمْ إِلَّا نُفُورًا ۝ قُل لَّوْ كَانَ مَعَهُۥٓ ءَالِهَةٌ كَمَا يَقُولُونَ إِذًا لَّٱبْتَغَوْا۟ إِلَىٰ ذِي ٱلْعَرْشِ سَبِيلًا ۝ سُبْحَٰنَهُۥ وَتَعَٰلَىٰ عَمَّا يَقُولُونَ عُلُوًّا كَبِيرًا ۝ تُسَبِّحُ لَهُ ٱلسَّمَٰوَٰتُ ٱلسَّبْعُ وَٱلْأَرْضُ وَمَن فِيهِنَّ ۚ وَإِن مِّن شَىْءٍ إِلَّا يُسَبِّحُ بِحَمْدِهِۦ وَلَٰكِن لَّا تَفْقَهُونَ تَسْبِيحَهُمْ ۗ إِنَّهُۥ كَانَ حَلِيمًا غَفُورًا ۝﴾

TAFSEER (EXPLANATION) OF THE VERSES

As your teacher reads the *Tafseer* of al-Imam as-Sa'dee (may Allah have Mercy on him), follow along carefully and take notes on the following points:

1. Providing many rulings and lessons:

2. The impact of that on sincere people:

   A.

   B.

3. Why do most people have an aversion to the Truth?

   A.

   B.

4. The actual response of most people:

5. How the foremost of all lessons, *towheed*, has been presented:

6. The effect of attentively listening to this:

7. One of the many rational arguments for *towheed*:

8. *"Say..."* (to whom?)

9. *"Had there been other deities [worthy of worship] along with Him..."*

10. *"They would certainly have sought nearness to the Owner of the Throne."*

11. The illogical nature of such a proposition

12. Other Verses with similar meanings:

    (17:57)

    (25:17-18)

13. Another possible explanation of Verse 42

    (23:91)

14. *"Exalted and Lofty He is, far above what they claim!"*

15. Exalted is He, and how needy is the entire creation!

16. Some of the ways the creation is in need of their Creator:

    A.

    B.

17. All things exalt Allah.

18. Yet we cannot understand their exaltations.

19. *"Truly, He is Ever Forbearing, Oft-Forgiving."*

LESSON 13

DISBELIEVERS DO NOT BENEFIT FROM THE QURAN

قال تعالى:

TODAY'S VERSES

45. And when you recite the Quran, We place a hidden barrier between you and those who do not believe in the Hereafter.

46. And We place coverings over their hearts, preventing them from understanding it, and in their ears deafness. Whenever you mention your Lord Alone in the Quran, they turn their backs, fleeing [in contempt].

47. We know best of what they listen to, when they listen to you, and when they take secret counsel, as the oppressive ones say: "You follow nothing but a bewitched man."

48. Consider the kinds of likenesses they attribute to you, while they go astray and are unable to find any path [of guidance].

﴿وَإِذَا قَرَأْتَ ٱلْقُرْءَانَ جَعَلْنَا بَيْنَكَ وَبَيْنَ ٱلَّذِينَ لَا يُؤْمِنُونَ بِٱلْءَاخِرَةِ حِجَابًا مَّسْتُورًا ۝ وَجَعَلْنَا عَلَىٰ قُلُوبِهِمْ أَكِنَّةً أَن يَفْقَهُوهُ وَفِىٓ ءَاذَانِهِمْ وَقْرًا وَإِذَا ذَكَرْتَ رَبَّكَ فِى ٱلْقُرْءَانِ وَحْدَهُۥ وَلَّوْاْ عَلَىٰٓ أَدْبَـٰرِهِمْ نُفُورًا ۝ نَّحْنُ أَعْلَمُ بِمَا يَسْتَمِعُونَ بِهِۦٓ إِذْ يَسْتَمِعُونَ إِلَيْكَ وَإِذْ هُمْ نَجْوَىٰٓ إِذْ يَقُولُ ٱلظَّـٰلِمُونَ إِن تَتَّبِعُونَ إِلَّا رَجُلًا مَّسْحُورًا ۝ ٱنظُرْ كَيْفَ ضَرَبُواْ لَكَ ٱلْأَمْثَالَ فَضَلُّواْ فَلَا يَسْتَطِيعُونَ سَبِيلًا ۝﴾

TAFSEER (EXPLANATION) OF THE VERSES

As your teacher reads the *Tafseer* of al-Imam as-Sa'dee (may Allah have Mercy on him), follow along carefully and take notes on the following points:

1. Allah informs us about how He punishes those who reject the Truth.

2. The actual meanings of the Quran (which they turn away from)

3. What this "hidden screen" does to them

4. The *"akinnah"* (أكنة) placed on their hearts

5. The *"waqr"* (وقر) placed in their ears

35

6. ***"Whenever you mention your Lord Alone in the Quran..."***

7. Why they turn away:

       A.

       B.

       (39:45)

8. What they actually intend when they do listen

9. Does listening benefit anyone when this is the intention?

10. Secret gatherings, ***"najwaa"*** (نجوى)

11. Where and when do the oppressive ones speak?

12. ***"You follow nothing but a bewitched man."***

13. Allah invites us to examine their claim, saying ***"Look/consider..."*** (انظر)

14. The likeness they described our Prophet with (صلى الله عليه وسلم)

15. How it led them astray

16. How they cannot even find a path to guidance

LESSON 14

THE FLAWED LOGIC & ARROGANCE OF DISBELIEVERS

TODAY'S VERSES   قَالَ تَعَالَى:

49. And they say: "When we are bones and scattered fragments, how could we really be resurrected as a new creation?"

50. Say: "Be you [objects made of] stones or iron,

51. Or some other created thing that is even greater in your breasts!" They will say: "Who could bring us back [to life]?" Say: "The One Who created you the first time!" Then, they will shake their heads at you [in disbelief] and say: "When will that be?" Say: "Perhaps it may be soon!"

52. On the Day when He calls you forth, and you respond with His praises. You will think that you have remained [in this worldly life] for only a short time.

TAFSEER (EXPLANATION) OF THE VERSES

As your teacher reads the *Tafseer* of al-Imam as-Sa'dee (may Allah have Mercy on him), follow along carefully and take notes on the following points:

1. *"When we are bones and scattered fragments..."*

2. Considering resurrection after death a logical impossibility

3. Analyzing the reality of this claim:

   A.

   B.

   C.

4. Allah shows us how foolish their thoughts are!

   (3:8)

5. ***"Be stones or iron..."*** That will not protect you, because:

    A.

    B.

6. You have nothing of *Ruboobiyyah* for yourselves

7. ***"They will say..."*** (When?)

8. The One who first created you will bring you back!

    (21:104)

9. The meaning of the shaking of their heads

10. The intent of the question, ***"When will that be?"***

11. Is it helpful to know exactly when the Day of Judgment will be?

12. ***"On the Day when He calls you forth..."***

13. You shall respond to Him with praises of Him.

14. The One to Whom praises are due

15. This entire worldly life will be like a short moment.

16. They are rebuked by what they used to deny and ridicule.

LESSON 15

ALLAH'S TRUE SERVANTS HAVE THE BEST SPEECH

قال تعالى:

TODAY'S VERSES

53. And say to My slaves that they must say [only] what is best, since the devil surely causes enmity between them. Indeed, the devil is a plain enemy to mankind.

54. Your Lord knows you best. If He wills, He will have mercy on you; if He wills, He will punish you. And We have not sent you (Muhammad) as a guardian over them.

55. And your Lord knows best about all who are in the heavens and on earth. We have surely preferred some prophets over others; to Daawood (David) We gave the *Zaboor* (Psalms).

﴿وَقُل لِّعِبَادِى يَقُولُوا۟ ٱلَّتِى هِىَ أَحْسَنُ إِنَّ ٱلشَّيْطَـٰنَ يَنزَغُ بَيْنَهُمْ إِنَّ ٱلشَّيْطَـٰنَ كَانَ لِلْإِنسَـٰنِ عَدُوًّۭا مُّبِينًۭا ۝ رَّبُّكُمْ أَعْلَمُ بِكُمْ إِن يَشَأْ يَرْحَمْكُمْ أَوْ إِن يَشَأْ يُعَذِّبْكُمْ وَمَآ أَرْسَلْنَـٰكَ عَلَيْهِمْ وَكِيلًۭا ۝ وَرَبُّكَ أَعْلَمُ بِمَن فِى ٱلسَّمَـٰوَٰتِ وَٱلْأَرْضِ وَلَقَدْ فَضَّلْنَا بَعْضَ ٱلنَّبِيِّـۧنَ عَلَىٰ بَعْضٍۢ وَءَاتَيْنَا دَاوُۥدَ زَبُورًۭا ۝﴾

TAFSEER (EXPLANATION) OF THE VERSES

As your teacher reads the *Tafseer* of al-Imam as-Sa'dee (may Allah have Mercy on him), follow along carefully and take notes on the following points:

1. From Allah's Kindness He orders His worshippers with only the best things.

2. Examples of good speech which Allah commands

1.	4.
2.	5.
3.	6.

3. When there are two possible good statements/actions for a situation:

    A.

    B.

4. What good speech leads to

39

5. The devil sows discord between Allah's worshippers.

6. The remedy for this problem:

    A.

    B.

7. The devil's main goal:

8. How to subdue him and thwart his efforts:

    A.

    B.

9. The end results of this struggle:

10. Contemplating that **"Allah knows best"**

    A. He wants:

    B. We may want:

11. Some get His Mercy, some get His punishment

    A.

    B.

12. The Prophet (صلى الله عليه وسلم) was not a **"wakeel"** (وكيل).

13. *"And your Lord knows best about all who are in the heavens and on earth..."*

14. Different ways some prophets were favored over others:

15. A specific example of that:

16. A point of reflection using sound logic:

LESSON 16

THE FUTILITY OF THOSE CALLED UPON BESIDES ALLAH

TODAY'S VERSES

قال تعالى:

﴿قُلِ ٱدْعُوا۟ ٱلَّذِينَ زَعَمْتُم مِّن دُونِهِۦ فَلَا يَمْلِكُونَ كَشْفَ ٱلضُّرِّ عَنكُمْ وَلَا تَحْوِيلًا ۝ أُو۟لَٰٓئِكَ ٱلَّذِينَ يَدْعُونَ يَبْتَغُونَ إِلَىٰ رَبِّهِمُ ٱلْوَسِيلَةَ أَيُّهُمْ أَقْرَبُ وَيَرْجُونَ رَحْمَتَهُۥ وَيَخَافُونَ عَذَابَهُۥٓ إِنَّ عَذَابَ رَبِّكَ كَانَ مَحْذُورًا ۝ وَإِن مِّن قَرْيَةٍ إِلَّا نَحْنُ مُهْلِكُوهَا قَبْلَ يَوْمِ ٱلْقِيَٰمَةِ أَوْ مُعَذِّبُوهَا عَذَابًا شَدِيدًا كَانَ ذَٰلِكَ فِى ٱلْكِتَٰبِ مَسْطُورًا ۝﴾

56. Say: "Call upon those besides Him whom you assume [to be worthy of worship]. They do not possess any power to remove adversity from you, or even to shift it in any way."

57. Those [objects of worship] whom they call upon are themselves seeking out ways to draw near to their Lord, hoping to be the closest [to Allah]. They hope for His Mercy and fear His Punishment. Verily, the Punishment of your Lord is ever something to be warned of!

58. And there is not a single village, except that We shall destroy it before the Day of Judgment, or punish it with a severe punishment. That is something written in the Book.

TAFSEER (EXPLANATION) OF THE VERSES

As your teacher reads the *Tafseer* of al-Imam as-Sa'dee (may Allah have Mercy on him), follow along carefully and take notes on the following points:

1. "Say…" to whom? And for what purpose?

    A.

    B.

2. *"Those… whom you assume…"*

3. They cannot prevent any harm from reaching you, like:

41

4. They cannot even **"shift"** the harm, meaning:

    A.

    B.

5. A rational conclusion based on sound logic

6. How broken their moral compass has become!

    A.

    B.

    (38:5)

7. Exposing the reality of those being called upon

8. What are they doing to draw near to Allah?

9. What their fear of Allah leads them to?

10. The punishment of your Lord

11. The great significance of these three kinds of worship:

12. The true sign of loving Allah:

13. Which type of **"village"** is being referred to here?

14. Destruction has been slated from Allah's Decree.

15. What this reminder should lead to

LESSON 17

STUBBORN REJECTION OF THE MOST AMAZING SIGNS

TODAY'S VERSES

قال تعالى:

59. And nothing prevents Us from sending *Aayaat* (proofs, evidences, signs, etc.), but that the people of old rejected them. We sent the she-camel to Thamood, as [a thing providing] insight and understanding, but they oppressed, by way of her. And We only sent the *Aayaat* (proofs, signs, etc.) as warnings to be feared.

60. And [remember] when We told you: "Verily! Your Lord has encompassed the people (i.e. there is nowhere to flee from Him)." And We only made the vision we showed you (Muhammad) as a trial for mankind, and likewise the cursed tree [*az-Zaqqoom*, as mentioned] in the Quran. We make them afraid, yet it only increases them in serious transgressions.

﴿وَمَا مَنَعَنَا أَن نُّرْسِلَ بِٱلْءَايَـٰتِ إِلَّآ أَن كَذَّبَ بِهَا ٱلْأَوَّلُونَ وَءَاتَيْنَا ثَمُودَ ٱلنَّاقَةَ مُبْصِرَةً فَظَلَمُوا۟ بِهَا وَمَا نُرْسِلُ بِٱلْءَايَـٰتِ إِلَّا تَخْوِيفًا ۝ وَإِذْ قُلْنَا لَكَ إِنَّ رَبَّكَ أَحَاطَ بِٱلنَّاسِ وَمَا جَعَلْنَا ٱلرُّءْيَا ٱلَّتِىٓ أَرَيْنَـٰكَ إِلَّا فِتْنَةً لِّلنَّاسِ وَٱلشَّجَرَةَ ٱلْمَلْعُونَةَ فِى ٱلْقُرْءَانِ وَنُخَوِّفُهُمْ فَمَا يَزِيدُهُمْ إِلَّا طُغْيَـٰنًا كَبِيرًا ۝﴾

TAFSEER (EXPLANATION) OF THE VERSES

As your teacher reads the *Tafseer* of al-Imam as-Sa'dee (may Allah have Mercy on him), follow along carefully and take notes on the following points:

1. The Mercy found in not providing **"aayaat aliqtiraah"** (آيات الاقتراح)

    Definition:

    Examples:

2. The **Sunnah** of Allah in dealing with rejection of such amazing signs

3. An example of an amazing sign sent to the people

4. Would they still be confused?

5. The wisdom in sending such signs

6. Allah has encompassed the people

7. The required reaction and response to this

8. The *ru'yaa* (الرؤيا) – What was it?

9. The cursed tree mentioned in the Quran

10. The intended point about these two trials

11. The wisdom in not mentioning some specific future affairs

12. *"We make them afraid, yet it only increases them in serious transgressions."*

LESSON 18

THE ORIGIN OF IBLEES' HATRED FOR MANKIND

TODAY'S VERSES

قال تعالى:

61. And [remember] when We said to the angels, "Prostrate to Adam." They all prostrated, but Iblees (the devil) did not. He said, "Shall I prostrate to someone You created from clay?"

62. He said, "Do you see this one whom You have honored more than me? If You allow me respite until the Day of Judgment, I will surely lead his offspring astray, all but a few!"

63. He (Allah) said: "Go then, and whoever of them follows you, then *Jahannam* will be your recompense, an ample compensation.

64. "Trick those of them you can trick with your voice, attack them with your cavalry and infantry, mutually share with them in wealth and children, and make them promises." Yet, the devil promises them nothing but deceit.

65. "Verily, My [true] slaves, you shall have no authority over them. And All-Sufficient is your Lord as a Guardian."

﴿وَإِذْ قُلْنَا لِلْمَلَٰٓئِكَةِ ٱسْجُدُوا۟ لِءَادَمَ فَسَجَدُوٓا۟ إِلَّآ إِبْلِيسَ قَالَ ءَأَسْجُدُ لِمَنْ خَلَقْتَ طِينًا ۝ قَالَ أَرَءَيْتَكَ هَٰذَا ٱلَّذِى كَرَّمْتَ عَلَىَّ لَئِنْ أَخَّرْتَنِ إِلَىٰ يَوْمِ ٱلْقِيَٰمَةِ لَأَحْتَنِكَنَّ ذُرِّيَّتَهُۥٓ إِلَّا قَلِيلًا ۝ قَالَ ٱذْهَبْ فَمَن تَبِعَكَ مِنْهُمْ فَإِنَّ جَهَنَّمَ جَزَآؤُكُمْ جَزَآءً مَّوْفُورًا ۝ وَٱسْتَفْزِزْ مَنِ ٱسْتَطَعْتَ مِنْهُم بِصَوْتِكَ وَأَجْلِبْ عَلَيْهِم بِخَيْلِكَ وَرَجِلِكَ وَشَارِكْهُمْ فِى ٱلْأَمْوَٰلِ وَٱلْأَوْلَٰدِ وَعِدْهُمْ وَمَا يَعِدُهُمُ ٱلشَّيْطَٰنُ إِلَّا غُرُورًا ۝ إِنَّ عِبَادِى لَيْسَ لَكَ عَلَيْهِمْ سُلْطَٰنٌ وَكَفَىٰ بِرَبِّكَ وَكِيلًا ۝﴾

TAFSEER (EXPLANATION) OF THE VERSES

As your teacher reads the *Tafseer* of al-Imam as-Sa'dee (may Allah have Mercy on him), follow along carefully and take notes on the following points:

1. Exposing the severe hatred of Iblees

2. Refusing to prostrate based on a false analogy

REVIEW: *SOORAH AL-A'RAAF* (7:12)

    A.

    B.

    C.

3. The devil's bold declaration

4. His exception of a few

5. Allah's response to Iblees

6. Iblees leads people astray by his voice.

7. The meaning of Iblees' cavalry and infantry

8. The meaning of these orders from Allah

9. Iblees gets a share of mankind's wealth and offspring. *How?*

    A.

    B.

    C.

    D.

    E.

10. The reality of the devil's promises

11. Examples of how he makes false promises:

    A.

    B.

    C.

12. Summary: What the devil wants & how to thwart him

13. Allah protects His true servants.

14. **"And All-Sufficient is your Lord as a Guardian."**

LESSON 19

ALLAH'S UNCHALLENGED LORDSHIP OVER THE CREATION

TODAY'S VERSES

قال تعالى:

66. Your Lord is the One Who enables the ship for you to sail through the sea, so that you might seek of His Bounty. Indeed, He is Ever Merciful to you all.

﴿رَبُّكُمُ ٱلَّذِى يُزْجِى لَكُمُ ٱلْفُلْكَ فِى ٱلْبَحْرِ لِتَبْتَغُوا۟ مِن فَضْلِهِۦٓ ۚ إِنَّهُۥ كَانَ بِكُمْ رَحِيمًا ۝

67. Whenever harm threatens you at sea, all those you call upon stray from you (i.e. you do not call upon any of them), except Him (Allah Alone). Yet, when He brings you safely to land, you turn away [from Him]. Mankind is ever so ungrateful!

وَإِذَا مَسَّكُمُ ٱلضُّرُّ فِى ٱلْبَحْرِ ضَلَّ مَن تَدْعُونَ إِلَّآ إِيَّاهُ ۖ فَلَمَّا نَجَّىٰكُمْ إِلَى ٱلْبَرِّ أَعْرَضْتُمْ ۚ وَكَانَ ٱلْإِنسَـٰنُ كَفُورًا ۝

68. Do you feel so secure that He would not cause a part of the land to swallow you up, or that He would not unleash upon you a violent sandstorm? You would then find no protector for yourselves!

أَفَأَمِنتُمْ أَن يَخْسِفَ بِكُمْ جَانِبَ ٱلْبَرِّ أَوْ يُرْسِلَ عَلَيْكُمْ حَاصِبًا ثُمَّ لَا تَجِدُوا۟ لَكُمْ وَكِيلًا ۝

69. Or do you feel so secure that He would not send you back a second time there [to the sea], and unleash upon you a hurricane of wind and drown you because of your disbelief? You would then not find any recourse against Us!

أَمْ أَمِنتُمْ أَن يُعِيدَكُمْ فِيهِ تَارَةً أُخْرَىٰ فَيُرْسِلَ عَلَيْكُمْ قَاصِفًا مِّنَ ٱلرِّيحِ فَيُغْرِقَكُم بِمَا كَفَرْتُمْ ۙ ثُمَّ لَا تَجِدُوا۟ لَكُمْ عَلَيْنَا بِهِۦ تَبِيعًا ۝

TAFSEER (EXPLANATION) OF THE VERSES

As your teacher reads the *Tafseer* of al-Imam as-Sa'dee (may Allah have Mercy on him), follow along carefully and take notes on the following points:

1. Reflecting over the great blessing of traveling by sea:

    A.

    B.

    C.

2. Another reminder about the Mercy of Allah

3. Momentary recognition and dedication

47

4. Neglect and abandonment, back to polytheism

5. The result of ignorance and ingratitude

6. Yet one who is knowledgeable and guided...

7. Ignorance, short-sightedness, and heedlessness

8. He is the same One who controls the dangers of the land.

9. But even if you only feared Him at sea...

10. A *"qaasif"* (قاصف) of wind

11. You would then have no *"tabee'"* (تبيع)

LESSON 20

THE CHILDREN OF ADAM HAVE BEEN TRULY HONORED

TODAY'S VERSES

قال تعالى:

70. Indeed, We have truly honored the children of Adam, and We have carried them on land and at sea. We have provided them with good, wholesome things, and We have preferred them over many of those whom We created, with distinguishing preference.

71. (Remember) the Day when We shall call forth all people along with their (respective) *imam* (i.e. leader, or book). Whoever is given his book in his right hand, such people shall read their books, and they will not be dealt with unjustly in the least.

72. And whoever is blind [to belief] in this world, such will be blind in the Hereafter, and even more astray.

﴿ وَلَقَدْ كَرَّمْنَا بَنِي ءَادَمَ وَحَمَلْنَٰهُمْ فِى ٱلْبَرِّ وَٱلْبَحْرِ وَرَزَقْنَٰهُم مِّنَ ٱلطَّيِّبَٰتِ وَفَضَّلْنَٰهُمْ عَلَىٰ كَثِيرٍ مِّمَّنْ خَلَقْنَا تَفْضِيلًا ۝ يَوْمَ نَدْعُواْ كُلَّ أُنَاسٍۭ بِإِمَٰمِهِمْ ۖ فَمَنْ أُوتِىَ كِتَٰبَهُۥ بِيَمِينِهِۦ فَأُوْلَٰٓئِكَ يَقْرَءُونَ كِتَٰبَهُمْ وَلَا يُظْلَمُونَ فَتِيلًا ۝ وَمَن كَانَ فِى هَٰذِهِۦٓ أَعْمَىٰ فَهُوَ فِى ٱلْءَاخِرَةِ أَعْمَىٰ وَأَضَلُّ سَبِيلًا ۝ ﴾

TAFSEER (EXPLANATION) OF THE VERSES

As your teacher reads the *Tafseer* of al-Imam as-Sa'dee (may Allah have Mercy on him), follow along carefully and take notes on the following points:

1. Allah favored human beings in many ways:

1.	4.
2.	5.
3.	6.

2. Allah granted us forms of transportation on land.

3. Allah granted us other forms of transportation at sea.

4. Many other wholesome provisions

5. No need left unfulfilled

6. **"And We have preferred them over many of those whom We created..."**

7. The grateful response to these blessings

8. The situation of the people when they are resurrected

9. Their records of deeds are compared to the books of their prophets.

10. Those who receive their records in their right hands

    A.

    B.

    C.

    D.

11. They read their books.

12. They are not oppressed.

13. What is the blameworthy blindness of this life?

14. What is the blindness of the Hereafter?

15. *"And even more astray"*

16. Summarizing some of the many proofs found in this Verse:

    A.

    B.

    C.

    D.

    E.

LESSON 21

EVEN PROPHETS NEED GUIDANCE & STABILITY FROM ALLAH

TODAY'S VERSES

قال تعالى:

73. Indeed, they plotted to divert you away from that which We have revealed to you (Muhammad), to fabricate something else from Us. They would certainly have taken you as a close friend [had they accomplished that]!

74. And had We not made you stand firm, you might have inclined towards them a little.

75. In that case, We would have made you taste a double portion [of punishment] in this life, as well as a double portion after dying. And then you would have found no one to help you against Us.

﴿وَإِن كَادُوا۟ لَيَفْتِنُونَكَ عَنِ ٱلَّذِىٓ أَوْحَيْنَآ إِلَيْكَ لِتَفْتَرِىَ عَلَيْنَا غَيْرَهُۥ ۖ وَإِذًا لَّٱتَّخَذُوكَ خَلِيلًا ۝ وَلَوْلَآ أَن ثَبَّتْنَٰكَ لَقَدْ كِدتَّ تَرْكَنُ إِلَيْهِمْ شَيْـًٔا قَلِيلًا ۝ إِذًا لَّأَذَقْنَٰكَ ضِعْفَ ٱلْحَيَوٰةِ وَضِعْفَ ٱلْمَمَاتِ ثُمَّ لَا تَجِدُ لَكَ عَلَيْنَا نَصِيرًا ۝﴾

TAFSEER (EXPLANATION) OF THE VERSES

As your teacher reads the *Tafseer* of al-Imam as-Sa'dee (may Allah have Mercy on him), follow along carefully and take notes on the following points:

1. A reminder about how Allah saved His Prophet (صلى الله عليه وسلم) from the people's plots

2. They wanted to trick him into changing what was revealed to him.

3. He would have become so dear to them, had they succeeded.

4. The real reason for their animosity

5. The blessing of stability in the face of plots

51

6. ***"You might have inclined towards them a little..."***

7. Allah saved him from punishment in both worlds

8. ***"And then you would have found no one to help you against Us."***

9. Yet Allah protected him and kept him from all types of corruption.

LESSON 22

MESSENGERS WERE ALWAYS EXPELLED FROM THEIR LANDS

TODAY'S VERSES

قال تعالى:

76. Indeed, they plotted to expel you from the land. In such a case, they would not remain after you, except for a little while.

77. [Such is] the *Sunnah* (way) of how We sent Our messengers before you (Muhammad); you will not find any change in Our *Sunnah*.

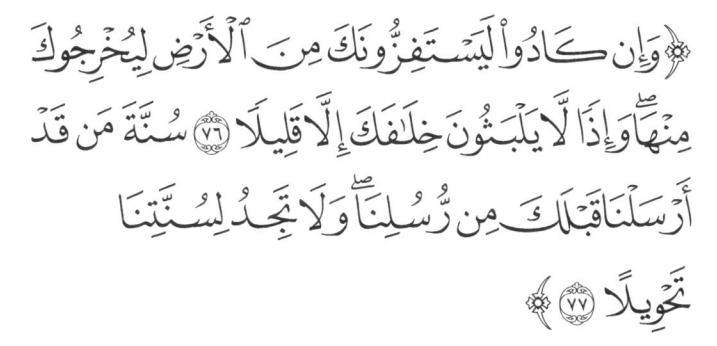

﴿وَإِن كَادُوا لَيَسْتَفِزُّونَكَ مِنَ ٱلْأَرْضِ لِيُخْرِجُوكَ مِنْهَا وَإِذًا لَّا يَلْبَثُونَ خِلَٰفَكَ إِلَّا قَلِيلًا ۝ سُنَّةَ مَن قَدْ أَرْسَلْنَا قَبْلَكَ مِن رُّسُلِنَا ۖ وَلَا تَجِدُ لِسُنَّتِنَا تَحْوِيلًا ۝﴾

TAFSEER (EXPLANATION) OF THE VERSES

As your teacher reads the *Tafseer* of al-Imam as-Sa'dee (may Allah have Mercy on him), follow along carefully and take notes on the following points:

1. The reason why they plotted to expel the Prophet (صلى الله عليه وسلم)

2. **"They would not remain after you..."**

3. The Sunnah of Allah with all the nations

4. This warning came to pass for the people of Makkah.

5. Mankind's severe need for Allah should lead him to:

    A.

    B.

6. Reflecting over the significance of these words directed to the Prophet (صلى الله عليه وسلم)

7. A reminder from Allah to His Prophet (صلى الله عليه وسلم)

8. Allah loves His slaves to recognize blessings

9. With great blessings there are higher standards to be fulfilled.

10. Insight into the Sunnah of Allah in how He destroys nations

LESSON 23

VICTORY AFTER SINCERE PRAYERS & SUPPLICATIONS

TODAY'S VERSES

78. Establish prayer once the sun passes its zenith [at mid-day], until the darkness of night, and then [recite] the Quran at dawn! Verily, [the recitation of] the Quran at dawn is ever witnessed!

79. At some parts of the night offer optional prayers, additional [rewards] for you (Muhammad); perhaps your Lord will send you forth to a praiseworthy station [of Intercession].

80. And say: "My Lord! Grant me an entry of honesty and an exit of honesty, and give me from Yourself a victory of aid and support (through proofs and evidences)."

81. And say: "The Truth has come, and falsehood has vanished. Surely, falsehood is ever fading away."

قال تعالى:

﴿أَقِمِ ٱلصَّلَوٰةَ لِدُلُوكِ ٱلشَّمْسِ إِلَىٰ غَسَقِ ٱلَّيْلِ وَقُرْءَانَ ٱلْفَجْرِ إِنَّ قُرْءَانَ ٱلْفَجْرِ كَانَ مَشْهُودًا ۝ وَمِنَ ٱلَّيْلِ فَتَهَجَّدْ بِهِۦ نَافِلَةً لَّكَ عَسَىٰٓ أَن يَبْعَثَكَ رَبُّكَ مَقَامًا مَّحْمُودًا ۝ وَقُل رَّبِّ أَدْخِلْنِي مُدْخَلَ صِدْقٍ وَأَخْرِجْنِي مُخْرَجَ صِدْقٍ وَٱجْعَل لِّي مِن لَّدُنكَ سُلْطَٰنًا نَّصِيرًا ۝ وَقُلْ جَآءَ ٱلْحَقُّ وَزَهَقَ ٱلْبَٰطِلُ إِنَّ ٱلْبَٰطِلَ كَانَ زَهُوقًا ۝﴾

TAFSEER (EXPLANATION) OF THE VERSES

As your teacher reads the *Tafseer* of al-Imam as-Sa'dee (may Allah have Mercy on him), follow along carefully and take notes on the following points:

1. Allah's command to His Prophet (صلى الله عليه وسلم) specifically

2. The *"dulook"* (دلوك) of the sun, which includes two prayers:

3. The *"ghasaq"* (غسق) of the night, which includes two prayers:

4. What is the **"Quran of Fajr"** (قرآن الفجر) & why is it called that?

    A.

    B.

5. All five daily prayers mentioned

6. The ruling on these five prayers

7. These specific times have two important relationships to that ruling:

    A.

    B.

8. This Verse indicates that some prayers can be combined in some circumstances.

9. Special things about Fajr Prayer:

    A.

    B.

    C.

10. **"At some parts of the night offer optional prayers..."**

11. How were night prayers **"naafilah"** (نافلة) for him?

12. Another way to understand this issue

13. What is the **"maqaam mahmood"** (مقام محمود)?

14. **"Grant me an entry of honesty and an exit of honesty..."**

15. What is the requested **"sultaan naseer"** (سلطان نصير)?

16. The best situation for any worshipper of Allah

17. What is the **"Truth"** which has come?

18. The Prophet (صلى الله عليه وسلم) was ordered to proclaim this.

19. The nature of falsehood

20. The importance of Islamic knowledge

LESSON 24

THE QURAN IS HEALING & MERCY FOR THE BELIEVERS

TODAY'S VERSES

قال تعالى:

82. And We send down among the Quran that which is a healing and a mercy to the believers, yet it does not increase the oppressive ones in anything but loss.

83. And whenever We bestow Our Grace on a [disbelieving] man, he arrogantly turns away, far away from the right path. Then, when evil reaches him he is ever in despair.

84. Say: "Each person behaves in line with his kind, and your Lord [Alone] knows best who is most guided to the right path."

﴿وَنُنَزِّلُ مِنَ ٱلْقُرْءَانِ مَا هُوَ شِفَآءٌ وَرَحْمَةٌ لِّلْمُؤْمِنِينَ وَلَا يَزِيدُ ٱلظَّٰلِمِينَ إِلَّا خَسَارًا ۝ وَإِذَآ أَنْعَمْنَا عَلَى ٱلْإِنسَٰنِ أَعْرَضَ وَنَـَٔا بِجَانِبِهِۦ وَإِذَا مَسَّهُ ٱلشَّرُّ كَانَ يَـُٔوسًا ۝ قُلْ كُلٌّ يَعْمَلُ عَلَىٰ شَاكِلَتِهِۦ فَرَبُّكُمْ أَعْلَمُ بِمَنْ هُوَ أَهْدَىٰ سَبِيلًا ۝﴾

TAFSEER (EXPLANATION) OF THE VERSES

As your teacher reads the *Tafseer* of al-Imam as-Sa'dee (may Allah have Mercy on him), follow along carefully and take notes on the following points:

1. The Quran's healing and mercy is not for everyone.

2. What the Quran does for oppressors and disbelievers

3. How the Quran heals sick hearts:

4. This healing extends from two basic components:

    A.

    B.

5. The Quran also heals the body (medically).

6. The way to obtain the Mercy of the Quran

57

7. The situation of most of mankind

8. Hopelessness in the face of difficulty

9. In contrast, the believer's situation is always good:

    A.

    B.

10. **"Say: Each person behaves in line with his kind..."**

    A.

    B.

11. Allah knows best who really deserves guidance.

LESSON 25

ASKING ABOUT THE ROOH WHILE REJECTING THE QURAN

TODAY'S VERSES

قال تعالى:

85. And they ask you about the *rooh* (the spirit or soul). Say: "The *rooh* is among the matters for my Lord [to know and potentially reveal information about]. And of knowledge, you (mankind) have only been given a little."

86. And had We so willed, We could have done away with what We had revealed to you. Then you would have found no protector for yourself against Us.

87. Except as a Mercy from your Lord. Verily, His Favor upon you is ever great!

88. Say: "If mankind and the Jinn came together to bring about the likes of this Quran, they could not produce its likes, even if they all supported one another."

﴿وَيَسْـَٔلُونَكَ عَنِ ٱلرُّوحِۖ قُلِ ٱلرُّوحُ مِنْ أَمْرِ رَبِّي وَمَآ أُوتِيتُم مِّنَ ٱلْعِلْمِ إِلَّا قَلِيلًا ۝ وَلَئِن شِئْنَا لَنَذْهَبَنَّ بِٱلَّذِيٓ أَوْحَيْنَآ إِلَيْكَ ثُمَّ لَا تَجِدُ لَكَ بِهِۦ عَلَيْنَا وَكِيلًا ۝ إِلَّا رَحْمَةً مِّن رَّبِّكَۚ إِنَّ فَضْلَهُۥ كَانَ عَلَيْكَ كَبِيرًا ۝ قُل لَّئِنِ ٱجْتَمَعَتِ ٱلْإِنسُ وَٱلْجِنُّ عَلَىٰٓ أَن يَأْتُوا۟ بِمِثْلِ هَٰذَا ٱلْقُرْءَانِ لَا يَأْتُونَ بِمِثْلِهِۦ وَلَوْ كَانَ بَعْضُهُمْ لِبَعْضٍ ظَهِيرًا ۝﴾

TAFSEER (EXPLANATION) OF THE VERSES

As your teacher reads the *Tafseer* of al-Imam as-Sa'dee (may Allah have Mercy on him), follow along carefully and take notes on the following points:

1. Censuring those who ask unnecessary questions

2. Asking about something unclear, while remaining ignorant of essential matters

3. **"The rooh is among the matters for my Lord..."**

4. An important manner for teachers and callers to Islam

5. Another reminder about the blessing of the Quran:

    A.

    B.

59

6. What would happen if it were taken away?

7. So then appreciate it, by doing three things:

> A.
>
> B.
>
> C.

8. Evidence for the truthfulness of our Prophet (صلى الله عليه وسلم)

9. How could mankind counter the Quran, while he is:

& How could they counter the Speech of Allah, while He is:

1.	4.
2.	5.
3.	6.

10. No one is comparable to Allah.

11. Rebuke of someone who could believe the Quran was invented by a person

LESSON 26

DISBELIEVERS STUBBORNLY DEMAND THINGS THEIR WAY

TODAY'S VERSES

قال تعالى:

89. Indeed, We have fully explained to mankind in this Quran every type of similitude, yet most people still refuse anything but disbelief.

90. And they have said, "We will not believe for you (Muhammad), until you cause a spring to gush forth from the earth for us;

91. Or you have a garden of date-palm trees and grapes, and you cause rivers to gush forth in their midst abundantly;

92. Or you cause the heavens to fall upon us in pieces, as you have claimed [might happen], or you bring Allah and the angels to us, face to face;

93. Or you have a house of adornments, or you ascend up into the sky! But we would still not believe in your ascension unless you brought down for us a Book to read ourselves." Say: "Exalted is my Lord! Am I anything but a man, [sent as] a messenger?"

94. And nothing ever prevented people from believing when guidance came to them, except that they said: "Has Allah sent a human being as a messenger?"

95. Say: "Had there been [only] angels walking about on earth in tranquility, We would certainly have sent down from the heavens an angel as a messenger for them."

96. Say: "Sufficient is Allah as a witness between me and you. Verily, He [Alone] is All-Knowing, All-Seeing, regarding His slaves."

﴿وَلَقَدْ صَرَّفْنَا لِلنَّاسِ فِى هَـٰذَا ٱلْقُرْءَانِ مِن كُلِّ مَثَلٍۢ فَأَبَىٰٓ أَكْثَرُ ٱلنَّاسِ إِلَّا كُفُورًۭا ۝ وَقَالُوا۟ لَن نُّؤْمِنَ لَكَ حَتَّىٰ تَفْجُرَ لَنَا مِنَ ٱلْأَرْضِ يَنۢبُوعًا ۝ أَوْ تَكُونَ لَكَ جَنَّةٌۭ مِّن نَّخِيلٍۢ وَعِنَبٍۢ فَتُفَجِّرَ ٱلْأَنْهَـٰرَ خِلَـٰلَهَا تَفْجِيرًا ۝ أَوْ تُسْقِطَ ٱلسَّمَآءَ كَمَا زَعَمْتَ عَلَيْنَا كِسَفًا أَوْ تَأْتِىَ بِٱللَّهِ وَٱلْمَلَـٰٓئِكَةِ قَبِيلًا ۝ أَوْ يَكُونَ لَكَ بَيْتٌۭ مِّن زُخْرُفٍ أَوْ تَرْقَىٰ فِى ٱلسَّمَآءِ وَلَن نُّؤْمِنَ لِرُقِيِّكَ حَتَّىٰ تُنَزِّلَ عَلَيْنَا كِتَـٰبًۭا نَّقْرَؤُهُۥ ۗ قُلْ سُبْحَانَ رَبِّى هَلْ كُنتُ إِلَّا بَشَرًۭا رَّسُولًۭا ۝ وَمَا مَنَعَ ٱلنَّاسَ أَن يُؤْمِنُوٓا۟ إِذْ جَآءَهُمُ ٱلْهُدَىٰٓ إِلَّآ أَن قَالُوٓا۟ أَبَعَثَ ٱللَّهُ بَشَرًۭا رَّسُولًۭا ۝ قُل لَّوْ كَانَ فِى ٱلْأَرْضِ مَلَـٰٓئِكَةٌۭ يَمْشُونَ مُطْمَئِنِّينَ لَنَزَّلْنَا عَلَيْهِم مِّنَ ٱلسَّمَآءِ مَلَكًۭا رَّسُولًۭا ۝ قُلْ كَفَىٰ بِٱللَّهِ شَهِيدًۢا بَيْنِى وَبَيْنَكُمْ ۚ إِنَّهُۥ كَانَ بِعِبَادِهِۦ خَبِيرًۢا بَصِيرًۭا ۝﴾

TAFSEER (EXPLANATION) OF THE VERSES

As your teacher reads the *Tafseer* of al-Imam as-Sa'dee (may Allah have Mercy on him), follow along carefully and take notes on the following points:

1. **"Indeed, We have fully explained to mankind in this Quran every type of similitude..."**

    A.

    B.

2. For what purpose was this done?

3. Who are the exempted minority (understood from **"Most people..."**)?

4. The majority insist on ingratitude.

5. An example of one of the disbelievers' stubborn demands: gushing water

6. Another example: a garden

7. Another example: Drop the sky on us!

8. Another example: Bring Allah and the angels to us!

9. Another example: a palace

10. Another example: ascending up into the sky

11. Blameworthy nature of these demands:

1.	4.
2.	5.
3.	6.

12. The order to exalt Allah:

    A.

    B.

13. **"Am I anything but a man, [sent as] a messenger?"**

14. A common problem mankind has had throughout the ages

15. A clear and rational explanation for why it is not appropriate

16. Allah as a witness for His prophet:

    A.

    B.

    C.

17. Allah did not allow any tampering with His message.

LESSON 27

REBUKE & PUNISHMENT OF THE DISBELIEVERS

TODAY'S VERSES

قال تعالى:

97. Whomever Allah guides, it is he who is rightly guided. Whomever He sends astray, for such you will find no allies [to help him] other than Him, and We shall gather them together on the Day of Judgment on their faces, blind, deaf, and dumb. Their abode will be *Jahannam*; every time it abates, We increase its blazing flames upon them.

98. That is their recompense, because they disbelieved in Our *Aayaat* (proofs, verses, signs, etc.) and said, "How could it be that after we are bones and fragments, we would really then be resurrected, as a new creation?"

99. Can they not see that Allah, the One Who created the heavens and the earth, is fully capable of creating their likes? And He has decreed for them an appointed term, about which there is no doubt. Yet, the oppressive people refuse everything but disbelief.

100. Say: "If you possessed the treasures of my Lord's Mercy, you would certainly hold back from spending in fear [of losing it]! Mankind is ever so miserly!"

﴿وَمَن يَهْدِ ٱللَّهُ فَهُوَ ٱلْمُهْتَدِ وَمَن يُضْلِلْ فَلَن تَجِدَ لَهُمْ أَوْلِيَآءَ مِن دُونِهِۦ وَنَحْشُرُهُمْ يَوْمَ ٱلْقِيَـٰمَةِ عَلَىٰ وُجُوهِهِمْ عُمْيًا وَبُكْمًا وَصُمًّا مَّأْوَىٰهُمْ جَهَنَّمُ كُلَّمَا خَبَتْ زِدْنَـٰهُمْ سَعِيرًا ۝ ذَٰلِكَ جَزَآؤُهُم بِأَنَّهُمْ كَفَرُوا۟ بِـَٔايَـٰتِنَا وَقَالُوٓا۟ أَءِذَا كُنَّا عِظَـٰمًا وَرُفَـٰتًا أَءِنَّا لَمَبْعُوثُونَ خَلْقًا جَدِيدًا ۝ أَوَلَمْ يَرَوْا۟ أَنَّ ٱللَّهَ ٱلَّذِى خَلَقَ ٱلسَّمَـٰوَٰتِ وَٱلْأَرْضَ قَادِرٌ عَلَىٰٓ أَن يَخْلُقَ مِثْلَهُمْ وَجَعَلَ لَهُمْ أَجَلًا لَّا رَيْبَ فِيهِ فَأَبَى ٱلظَّـٰلِمُونَ إِلَّا كُفُورًا ۝ قُل لَّوْ أَنتُمْ تَمْلِكُونَ خَزَآئِنَ رَحْمَةِ رَبِّىٓ إِذًا لَّأَمْسَكْتُمْ خَشْيَةَ ٱلْإِنفَاقِ وَكَانَ ٱلْإِنسَـٰنُ قَتُورًا ۝﴾

TAFSEER (EXPLANATION) OF THE VERSES

As your teacher reads the *Tafseer* of al-Imam as-Sa'dee (may Allah have Mercy on him), follow along carefully and take notes on the following points:

1. Whomever Allah guides:

    A.

    B.

    C.

2. Whomever Allah misguides:

3. **"We shall gather them... on their faces, blind, deaf, and dumb..."**

4. Their place of dwelling will be *Jahannam*.

5. **"Every time it abates, We increase its blazing flames upon them..."**

   A.

   B.

   C.

6. Allah does not oppress them, He only recompenses them for what they did:

   A.

   B.

   C.

7. **"After we are bones and fragments, we would really then be resurrected...?"**

8. Considering the creation of the heavens and earth comparatively

9. Responding to the Quran's rhetorical questions

10. Respite is given until an appointed term.

11. **"Yet, the oppressive people refuse everything but disbelief..."**

12. The treasures of Allah's Mercy

13. Just because mankind is so miserly...!

LESSON 28

MORE IMPORTANT LESSONS FROM PHARAOH'S STORY

TODAY'S VERSES

قال تعالى:

101. And indeed We gave Moosaa (Moses) nine clear signs. Ask the Children of Israel about when he came to them and Pharaoh said to him: "O Moosaa (Moses)! I think you are indeed bewitched."

102. He (Moosaa) said: "Surely, you know that these signs have been sent down by none other than Lord of the heavens and the earth as clear evidences, providing knowledge and insight! And so I think it is you, O Pharaoh, who is actually doomed to destruction!"

103. So he (Pharaoh) wanted to exile them (Moosaa and the Children of Israel) out of the land, but We drowned him (Pharaoh) instead, along with everyone with him.

104. And We said to the Children of Israel after him: "Dwell in the land now, and when the final promise comes, We shall bring you all together!"

105. With truth We sent it (the Quran) down, and with truth it has come down. And We have only sent you (Muhammad) as a bearer of glad tidings and a warner.

﴿ وَلَقَدْ ءَاتَيْنَا مُوسَىٰ تِسْعَ ءَايَٰتٍۭ بَيِّنَٰتٍۖ فَسْـَٔلْ بَنِىٓ إِسْرَٰٓءِيلَ إِذْ جَآءَهُمْ فَقَالَ لَهُۥ فِرْعَوْنُ إِنِّى لَأَظُنُّكَ يَٰمُوسَىٰ مَسْحُورًا ۝ قَالَ لَقَدْ عَلِمْتَ مَآ أَنزَلَ هَٰٓؤُلَآءِ إِلَّا رَبُّ ٱلسَّمَٰوَٰتِ وَٱلْأَرْضِ بَصَآئِرَ وَإِنِّى لَأَظُنُّكَ يَٰفِرْعَوْنُ مَثْبُورًا ۝ فَأَرَادَ أَن يَسْتَفِزَّهُم مِّنَ ٱلْأَرْضِ فَأَغْرَقْنَٰهُ وَمَن مَّعَهُۥ جَمِيعًا ۝ وَقُلْنَا مِنۢ بَعْدِهِۦ لِبَنِىٓ إِسْرَٰٓءِيلَ ٱسْكُنُوا۟ ٱلْأَرْضَ فَإِذَا جَآءَ وَعْدُ ٱلْءَاخِرَةِ جِئْنَا بِكُمْ لَفِيفًا ۝ وَبِٱلْحَقِّ أَنزَلْنَٰهُ وَبِٱلْحَقِّ نَزَلَۗ وَمَآ أَرْسَلْنَٰكَ إِلَّا مُبَشِّرًا وَنَذِيرًا ۝ ﴾

TAFSEER (EXPLANATION) OF THE VERSES

As your teacher reads the *Tafseer* of al-Imam as-Sa'dee (may Allah have Mercy on him), follow along carefully and take notes on the following points:

1. **Divine consolation:** You are not the first messenger to be rejected and oppressed.

2. The nine clear signs:

1.	6.
2.	7.
3.	8.
4.	9.
5.	

3. If there is any doubt about that, then:

4. Moosaa exposes the reality of Pharaoh's statement.

5. **"And so I think it is you, O Pharaoh, who is actually doomed to destruction!"**

6. So then Pharaoh wants to exile them.

7. The drowning of Pharaoh and his army

8. **"When the final promise comes, We shall bring you all together..."**

9. Allah sent down the Quran in truth, in order to:

10. With truth, it came down:

11. A summary of the mission of the Prophet (صلى الله عليه وسلم)

    A.

    B.

LESSON 29

HOW TRUE BELIEVERS INTERACT WITH THE QURAN

قال تعالى:

TODAY'S VERSES

106. And [it is] a Quran which We have divided into parts, so that you (Muhammad) would recite it to the people over time. And We have sent it down in stages of revelation.

107. Say: "Believe in it (the Quran), or do not believe. Verily, those who were given knowledge before it, when it is recited to them, they fall down on their faces in prostration."

108. And they say: "Exalted is our Lord! The Promise of our Lord will be enacted."

109. And they fall down on their faces weeping, and it increases them in humility.

﴿ وَقُرْءَانًا فَرَقْنَٰهُ لِتَقْرَأَهُۥ عَلَى ٱلنَّاسِ عَلَىٰ مُكْثٍ وَنَزَّلْنَٰهُ تَنزِيلًا ۝ قُلْ ءَامِنُوا۟ بِهِۦٓ أَوْ لَا تُؤْمِنُوٓا۟ إِنَّ ٱلَّذِينَ أُوتُوا۟ ٱلْعِلْمَ مِن قَبْلِهِۦٓ إِذَا يُتْلَىٰ عَلَيْهِمْ يَخِرُّونَ لِلْأَذْقَانِ سُجَّدًا ۝ وَيَقُولُونَ سُبْحَٰنَ رَبِّنَآ إِن كَانَ وَعْدُ رَبِّنَا لَمَفْعُولًا ۝ وَيَخِرُّونَ لِلْأَذْقَانِ يَبْكُونَ وَيَزِيدُهُمْ خُشُوعًا ۩ ۝ ﴾

TAFSEER (EXPLANATION) OF THE VERSES

As your teacher reads the *Tafseer* of al-Imam as-Sa'dee (may Allah have Mercy on him), follow along carefully and take notes on the following points:

1. The **"division"** of the Quran

    A.

    B.

2. The benefit of reciting it in parts over time:

3. *"And We have sent it down in stages of revelation..."*

4. *"Say..."* to whom?

5. Whether you believe in it or not:

67

6. Allah has worshippers who are deeply affected by the Quran.

7. His worshippers exalt Him

8. The promise of Allah is surely true.

9. *"And they fall down on their faces weeping, and it increases them in humility."*

10. This is a description of the true believers from *Ahlul-Kitaab* (Jews & Christians)

FURTHER READING & RESEARCH: *Compare the modern "interfaith" approach that some Muslims employ when speaking to Jews and Christians to the actual Quranic method of inviting them to worship none but Allah, found throughout the Noble Quran. Give special attention to Soorah al-Maa'idah, especially Verses 72-77.*

LESSON 30

EXALT & PRAISE ALLAH IN YOUR PRAYERS & SUPPLICATIONS

TODAY'S VERSES

قال تعالى:

110. Say: "Call upon Allah, or call upon *ar-Rahmaan* (the Most Gracious). Whichever [name] you call upon Him with, to Him belong the most beautiful Names." And do not be too loud in your prayers, nor be too quiet in them; instead seek a middle course between those ways.

111. And say: "All praise is due to Allah [Alone], the One Who has not taken a son, nor does He have any partner in (His) Sovereignty, nor does He have any caretaker because of weakness." And declare His Greatness with pure declarations.

﴿قُلِ ٱدْعُوا۟ ٱللَّهَ أَوِ ٱدْعُوا۟ ٱلرَّحْمَـٰنَ ۖ أَيًّا مَّا تَدْعُوا۟ فَلَهُ ٱلْأَسْمَآءُ ٱلْحُسْنَىٰ ۚ وَلَا تَجْهَرْ بِصَلَاتِكَ وَلَا تُخَافِتْ بِهَا وَٱبْتَغِ بَيْنَ ذَٰلِكَ سَبِيلًا ۝ وَقُلِ ٱلْحَمْدُ لِلَّهِ ٱلَّذِى لَمْ يَتَّخِذْ وَلَدًا وَلَمْ يَكُن لَّهُۥ شَرِيكٌ فِى ٱلْمُلْكِ وَلَمْ يَكُن لَّهُۥ وَلِىٌّ مِّنَ ٱلذُّلِّ ۖ وَكَبِّرْهُ تَكْبِيرًا ۝﴾

TAFSEER (EXPLANATION) OF THE VERSES

As your teacher reads the *Tafseer* of al-Imam as-Sa'dee (may Allah have Mercy on him), follow along carefully and take notes on the following points:

1. Whichever Name you mention, His are the most beautiful Names.

2. Choosing the most appropriate Name for each situation

3. *"And do not be too loud in your prayers, nor be too quiet in them..."*

    A.

    B.

4. Seeking a middle course between those ways

5. A command to praise Allah

6. The Sovereign Lord without any son or partner

7. *"Nor does He have any caretaker because of weakness..."*

8. Declare His Greatness:

    A.

    B.

    C.

    D.

9. Concluding the explanation of *Soorah al-Israa'* & dating its completion

AL-HAMDU LILLAAH

All praise is due to Allah! This completes our study of these 111 beautiful verses of this amazing chapter, *Soorah al-Israa'*. May Allah accept these efforts of ours, as well as our fasting and praying, and may He forgive our sins and allow us entrance to His Paradise. Indeed, His Promise is true!

﴿ إِنَّ ٱلَّذِينَ ءَامَنُواْ وَعَمِلُواْ ٱلصَّٰلِحَٰتِ يَهۡدِيهِمۡ رَبُّهُم بِإِيمَٰنِهِمۡۖ تَجۡرِي مِن تَحۡتِهِمُ ٱلۡأَنۡهَٰرُ فِي جَنَّٰتِ ٱلنَّعِيمِ ۝ دَعۡوَىٰهُمۡ فِيهَا سُبۡحَٰنَكَ ٱللَّهُمَّ وَتَحِيَّتُهُمۡ فِيهَا سَلَٰمٌۚ وَءَاخِرُ دَعۡوَىٰهُمۡ أَنِ ٱلۡحَمۡدُ لِلَّهِ رَبِّ ٱلۡعَٰلَمِينَ ۝ ﴾

سورة يونس

Verily those who have believed and worked righteous deeds, their Lord guides them by their faith. Rivers flow from under them in gardens of joy. Their call therein is: *"Subhaanak Allaahumma"* (Exalted You are, O Allah). And their greeting therein is *salaam* (peace). And the last of their call is: "All praise is due to Allah, Lord of all things." [10:9-10]

ٱلۡحَمۡدُ لِلَّهِ
رَبِّ ٱلۡعَٰلَمِينَ

HOW TO ACCESS THE FREE CLASS RECORDINGS & AUDIO RESOURCES

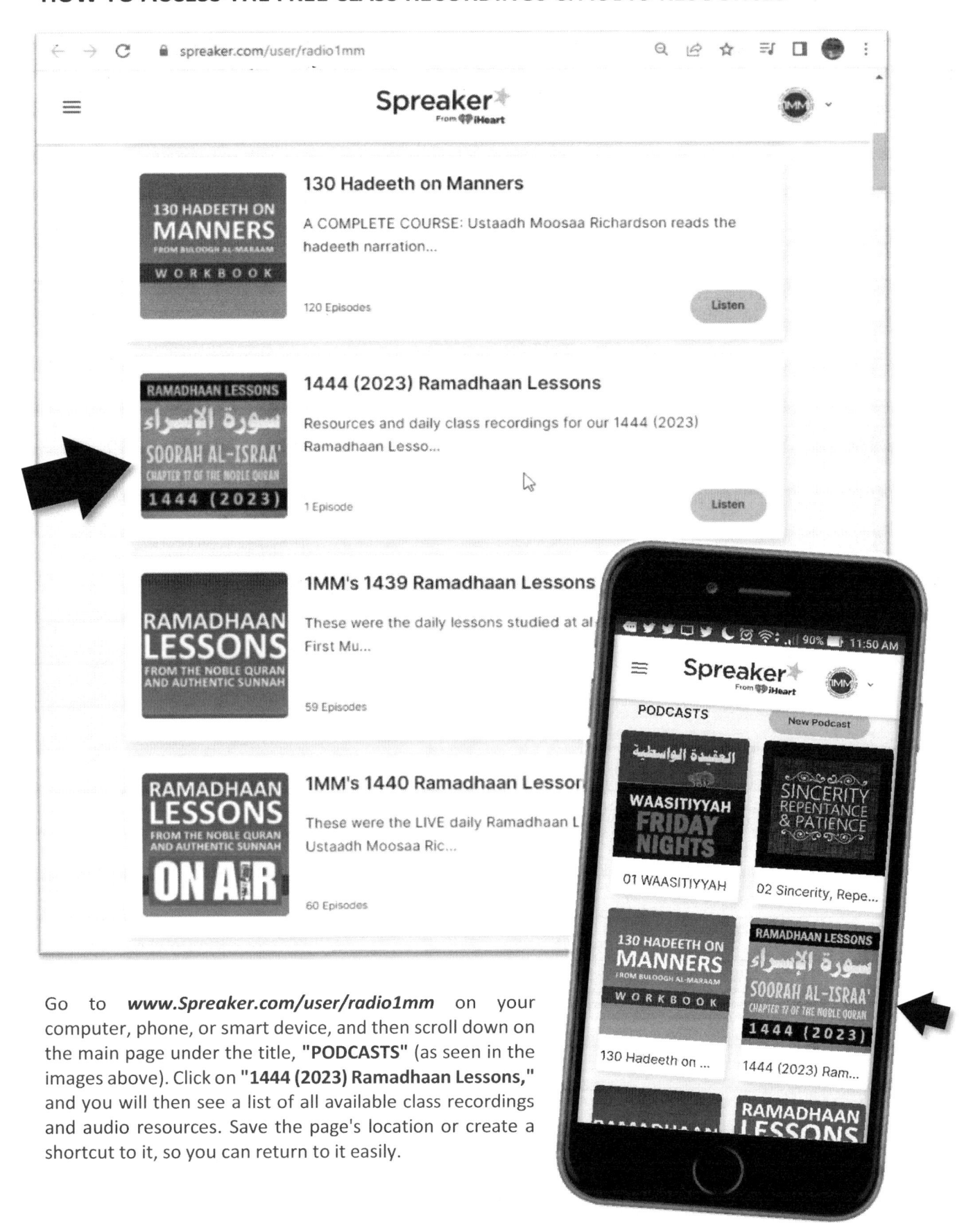

Go to **www.Spreaker.com/user/radio1mm** on your computer, phone, or smart device, and then scroll down on the main page under the title, **"PODCASTS"** (as seen in the images above). Click on **"1444 (2023) Ramadhaan Lessons,"** and you will then see a list of all available class recordings and audio resources. Save the page's location or create a shortcut to it, so you can return to it easily.

72

QUIZ 1

REVIEW OF WEEK 1: LESSONS 1-7 (VERSES 1-25)

QUIZ 1: REVIEW QUESTIONS

The following questions are designed to test your understanding of the first 25 Verses of Soorah al-Israa' and the explanation of al-Imam as-Sa'dee. After taking the quiz on your own, check your answers with the Answer Key on p.84.

1. Is S*oorah al-Israa'* classified by al-Imam as-Sa'dee as *Makkiyyah* or *Madaniyyah*?
    A. *Makkiyyah*
    B. *Madaniyyah*
    C. The verses of this *soorah* are equally distributed between the two categories.
    D. Neither; this *soorah* was revealed in Palestine.

2. What is the difference between *Makkee* and *Madanee* passages of the Quran?
    A. *Makkee* verses were revealed in Makkah, *Madanee* verses in Madeenah.
    B. *Makkee* verses warn about the hypocrites and the Last Day specifically.
    C. *Madanee* verses focus primarily on stories.
    D. *Makkee* verses were revealed before *Hijrah*; *Madanee* afterwards.

3. Which name does al-Imam as-Sa'dee use to refer to this *soorah*?
    A. *Soorah al-Israa'*
    B. *Soorah Banee Israa'eel*
    C. Both A and B
    D. Neither A nor B

4. What does **"al-Masjid al-Haraam"** in Verse #1 refer to, according to al-Imam as-Sa'dee?
    A. the sacred city of Makkah
    B. the sacred masjid in Makkah (i.e. the Ka'bah)
    C. the Prophet's masjid in al-Madeenah (صلى الله عليه وسلم)
    D. the sacred masjid in Palestine

5. Was the Prophet (صلى الله عليه وسلم) taken up to the heavens in a dream or in real life?
    A. in a dream state, with both his body and soul
    B. while awake, with both his body and soul
    C. while awake, with only his soul, not his actual body
    D. in a dream state, with only his body, not his soul

6. Who were decreed to cause corruption two times, as mentioned in Verse #3?
    A. the Children of Israel
    B. the descendants of Adam
    C. the *Ummah* of Nooh
    D. the civilizations of 'Aad and Thamood

73

7. Which of the following descriptions was **NOT** mentioned by al-Imam as-Sa'dee as one of the ways the faces of the Children of Israel were made sorrowful?

    A. They would be conquered.
    B. They would be taken as captives.
    C. Their opponents would enter the masjid.
    D. They would be barred from entering the masjid.

8. Which example does al-Imam as-Sa'dee provide for mankind supplicating against himself with evil, as much as he supplicates for good?

    A. A man supplicates against himself, his children, and his wealth.
    B. A man supplicates against his own wife and close relatives.
    C. A man supplicates against his closest companions.
    D. all of the above

9. Who will be told on the Day of Judgment, *"Read your book. You yourself are sufficient as a reckoner against you on this Day"*?

    A. the Children of Israel specifically
    B. the descendants of Adam generally
    C. the disbelievers exclusively
    D. the true believers exclusively

10. Which duty does Allah mention secondly, only after the obligation of worshipping Him alone, in the 23rd Verse of *Soorah al-Israa'*?

    A. the obligation of caring for orphans
    B. dutifulness to parents
    C. the obligation of the five daily prayers
    D. financial responsibilities, like paying *zakaat*

ANSWER KEY: See p.84

QUIZ 2

REVIEW OF WEEK 2: LESSONS 8-14 (VERSES 26-52)

QUIZ 2: REVIEW QUESTIONS

The following questions are designed to test your understanding of Verses 26-52 of Soorah al-Israa' and the explanation of al-Imam as-Sa'dee. After taking the quiz on your own, check your answers with the Answer Key on p.84.

1. People who waste their wealth are considered brothers of:

    A. Pharaoh
    B. the Children of Israel
    C. the devils
    D. hypocrites

2. Which of the following was **NOT** mentioned by as-Sa'dee as one of the harms of *zinaa*?

    A. the spread of diseases
    B. corruption of lineage
    C. violating the wife's rights
    D. corrupting the marriage

3. The heir of the murder victim has been granted **sultaan** (authority) to do what?

    A. seek the death penalty for the killer through the Islamic courts
    B. take the life of any of the killer's family members he so chooses
    C. take a share of the inheritance of the killer
    D. allow the killer entrance to Paradise or not

4. Which of the following was specifically mentioned by al-Imam as-Sa'dee as something which is **NOT** permissible when seeking the death penalty in Islamic Law?

    A. requesting the killer and his family to be exiled
    B. requesting that the killer be jailed for life instead of capital punishment
    C. forgiving the killer completely
    D. requesting the killer to be mutilated when put to death

5. Which of the following ways of interacting with the orphan's wealth is **permissible**?

    A. investing it in risky investments
    B. taking it as a service fee for orphan care
    C. increasing it with wise investments
    D. all of the above

6. The polytheists of Makkah assumed which of the following things?

    A. that Allah gave them daughters and kept sons for Himself
    B. that Allah gave them sons and kept daughters for Himself
    C. that Allah did not create them or their forefathers
    D. that Allah never provided for them at all

7. What rational argument does Allah provide for those who claim that He actually has partners who are worthy of worship?
    A. Had that been the case, such deities would have sought nearness to Allah.
    B. If that were true, they would all have sent prophets and messengers.
    C. Worship directed to them would ultimately reach Allah anyway.
    D. Prophets and messengers have more right to be worshipped.

8. What does Allah mention as the result of the pagans claiming that Muslims only follow a man who had magic spells put on him?
    A. They will be made to wear cloaks of iron and brass in the Hellfire.
    B. They are astray and cannot find any path of guidance.
    C. Magic spells will be put on them in this life and in the Hereafter.
    D. Their idols will be incapable of protecting them from magic spells.

9. What is the explanation of the Verse [which means]: **"They will shake their heads at you and say, 'When will that be?'"**
    A. People genuinely ask when the Day of Judgment will be.
    B. Pagans in Makkah ask when the conquering of Makkah would happen.
    C. Disbelievers arrogantly reject belief in the Day of Judgment.
    D. The Jews mock the Muslims about their plans to conquer Rome soon.

10. Complete the meaning of the Verse from *Soorah al-Israa'*: **"On the Day when He calls you forth, and you respond with _____."**
    A. curses upon yourselves and your families for being disbelievers
    B. hearts begging for His Forgiveness and Mercy
    C. obedience and submission
    D. praises of Him

ANSWER KEY: See p.84

QUIZ 3

REVIEW OF WEEK 3: LESSONS 15-21 (VERSES 53-75)

QUIZ 3: REVIEW QUESTIONS

The following questions are designed to test your understanding of Verses 53-75 of Soorah al-Israa' and the explanation of al-Imam as-Sa'dee. After taking the quiz on your own, check your answers with the Answer Key on p.84.

1. Allah says [what means]: **"And say to My slaves that they must say [only] what is best..."** Which of the following did al-Imam as-Sa'dee **NOT** mention as a specific example of this?
    A. ordering good
    B. *naseehah* (advice)
    C. remembrance (*thikr*)
    D. forbidding evil

2. How did al-Imam as-Sa'dee explain Allah's Statement [which means], **"And We have not sent you (Muhammad) as a wakeel (guardian) over them..."**?
    A. You are not in control of their affairs, nor do you recompense them.
    B. Allah is the only Wakeel over them.
    C. You are only someone who conveys a message and guides.
    D. all of the above

3. Which of the following distinctions between the prophets is **NOT TRUE**?
    A. Some had more followers than others.
    B. Some had more virtues than others.
    C. Some were weak in faith; others were strong.
    D. Some had books of revelation; others did not.

4. Allah negated that false deities can remove harm from their worshippers, nor can they "shift" that harm. What did al-Imam as-Sa'dee explain this "shift" to mean?
    A. Shifting it from one person to another
    B. Shifting it from one land to another
    C. Shifting it from one era of time to another
    D. all of the above

5. Al-Imam as-Sa'dee mentioned that the sign of someone truly loving Allah is:
    A. exerting oneself in sincere acts of worship
    B. advising people to travel for Hajj specifically
    C. worshipping Allah continually with all forms of worship known to mankind
    D. none of the above

6. To which civilization did Allah send the she-camel as a sign?
    A. 'Aad
    B. Thamood
    C. Ancient Egypt
    D. Rome

7. What is the name of the cursed tree, as mentioned in the Quran?
    A. The name of the tree is not mentioned in the Quran.
    B. *al-Buraaq*
    C. *az-Zaqqoom*
    D. *al-Jaheem*

8. How did al-Imam as-Sa'dee explain that Iblees was granted permission to **"Share with them (humans) in wealth and children,"** as mentioned in the 64th Verse?
    A. earning impermissible income
    B. male Jinn having intercourse with some human women
    C. wearing gold and silk (for men)
    D. all of the above

9. Which of the following did al-Imam as-Sa'dee **NOT** mention among his examples of how Allah has favored the children of Adam, in explanation of the 70th Verse?
    A. intellect
    B. knowledge
    C. giving them the ability to travel by sea
    D. send them books and messengers

10. The people will all be gathered with their *"imams"* on the Day of Judgment, as mentioned in Verse 71. How did al-Imam as-Sa'dee explain the word *"imam"*?
    A. their messengers and the representatives of those messengers
    B. their individual record books of deeds
    C. their local governmental authorities
    D. their books of revelation that were sent to them as guidance

ANSWER KEY: See p.84.

QUIZ 4

REVIEW OF WEEK 4: LESSONS 22-28 (VERSES 76-100)

QUIZ 4: REVIEW QUESTIONS

The following questions are designed to test your understanding of Verses 76-100 of Soorah al-Israa' and the explanation of al-Imam as-Sa'dee. After taking the quiz on your own, check your answers with the Answer Key on p.84.

1. Allah says [what means], **"Indeed, they plotted to expel you from the land."** How did al-Imam as-Sa'dee explain this Verse?

    A. The pagans of Makkah actually expelled the believers from Makkah
    B. The Jews of al-Madeenah were unable to expel the believers from al-Madeenah.
    C. The Jews of al-Madeenah actually expelled the believers from al-Madeenah.
    D. The pagans of Makkah plotted to expel the believers from al-Madeenah.

2. Which of the five daily prayers are included in the Statement of Allah [which means], **"Establish prayers once the sun passes its zenith, until the darkness of night, and then [recite] the Quran at dawn"**?

    A. only *Thuhr*, *'Eshaa'*, and *Fajr*
    B. all five of them
    C. Only *Thuhr* and *'Eshaa'*
    D. none of them

3. What is the **"maqaam mahmood"** which our Prophet (صلى الله عليه وسلم) was encouraged to strive for, as explained by al-Imam as-Sa'dee?

    A. the great intercession on the Day of Judgment
    B. interceding for the believers in this life and the Next Life
    C. his *howdh* (pool) on the Day of Judgment
    D. all of the above

4. Al-Imam as-Sa'dee explained that the "healing" of the Quran is:

    A. exclusive to physical illness
    B. exclusive to spiritual illness
    C. applicable to illnesses of both the heart and the body
    D. only for illnesses of the heart

5. When the people asked our Prophet (صلى الله عليه وسلم) about the *"rooh,"* Allah revealed:

    A. That the *"rooh"* is Jibreel.
    B. That they cannot ask any more religious questions for a period of 50 days.
    C. That knowledge of the *"rooh"* is not beneficial.
    D. none of the above

6. Who is being addressed in the Verse that means, **"And of knowledge, <u>YOU</u> have only been given a little..."**
  A. the Prophet Muhammad (صلى الله عليه وسلم)
  B. the Persians specifically
  C. the disbelievers who asked about the *"rooh"*
  D. the Jews specifically

7. Al-Imam as-Sa'dee extracted which of the following educational techniques from the question about the *"rooh"* and the answer provided by Allah?
  A. only teaching religious matters which are asked about, when they are asked
  B. answering religious questions during a journey, even while mounted
  C. ignoring difficult questions entirely, without providing any answer at all
  D. shifting the focus of misguided questioners to what is more beneficial for them

8. Which of the following was **NOT** one of the demands of the disbelievers, as cited in *Soorah al-Israa'*?
  A. The Prophet should bring the sky down upon them.
  B. The Prophet should bring Allah and the angels to the people.
  C. The Prophet should split the moon in half.
  D. The Prophet should have a garden with date-palm trees and grapes.

9. Allah exposes that if the disbelievers possessed the treasures of Allah's Mercy:
  A. Then, and only then, would they become generous.
  B. They would still be miserly.
  C. They would spend on themselves lavishly.
  D. all of the above

10. Which of the following is **NOT** one of the nine clear signs given to Moosaa?
  A. the staff
  B. frogs
  C. splitting the sea
  D. monkeys

ANSWER KEY: See p.84

QUIZ 5

REVIEW OF SOORAH AL-ISRAA' (VERSES 1-111) & ITS TAFSEER

QUIZ: COMPREHENSIVE REVIEW QUESTIONS

The following questions are designed to test your understanding of Soorah al-Israa' and the explanation of al-Imam as-Sa'dee. After taking the quiz on your own, check your answers with the Answer Key on p.84.

1. What other name does al-Imam as-Sa'dee use to refer to *Soorah al-Israa'*?

   A. *Soorah Banee al-Israa'*
   B. *Soorah Banee Israa'eel*
   C. *Soorah al-Mi'raaj*
   D. *Soorah al-Furqaan*

2. What does **"al-Masjid al-Haraam"** in Verse #1 refer to, according to al-Imam as-Sa'dee?

   A. the entire region of *Shaam* (the Levantine)
   B. the sacred masjid in Makkah (i.e. the Ka'bah)
   C. the Prophet's masjid in al-Madeenah (صلى الله عليه وسلم)
   D. the entire city of Makkah

3. Was the Prophet (صلى الله عليه وسلم) taken up to the heavens while awake or sleeping?

   A. in a dream state, with both his body and soul
   B. while awake, with both his body and soul
   C. while sleeping, with only his soul, not his actual body
   D. in a dream state, with only his body, not his soul

4. Which of the following descriptions was mentioned by al-Imam as-Sa'dee as one of the ways the faces of the Children of Israel were made sorrowful?

   A. Their harvests would bear no fruits for seven years.
   B. They would be taken as captives.
   C. Their opponents would enter a peace treaty with them.
   D. They would be barred from entering the masjid.

5. Which example does al-Imam as-Sa'dee provide for mankind supplicating against himself with evil, as much as he supplicates for good?

   A. A man supplicates against himself.
   B. A man supplicates against his children.
   C. A man supplicates against his wealth.
   D. all of the above

6. Which religious obligation does Allah mention secondly, only after the duty of worshipping Him alone, in the 23rd Verse of *Soorah al-Israa'*?
   A. the obligation of caring for stranded travelers
   B. offering the five daily prayers
   C. dutifulness to parents
   D. paying *zakaat*

7. Which of the following was mentioned by as-Sa'dee as one of the harms of *zinaa*?
   A. the spread of disease
   B. corruption of lineage
   C. violating the orphan's rights
   D. the spread of homosexuality

8. The heir of the murder victim has been granted **sultaan** (authority) to do what?
   A. jail the murderer for his entire life
   B. take the life of any of the killer's family members he so chooses
   C. take the entire inheritance of the killer
   D. seek the death penalty for the killer or excuse him

9. Which of the following ways of interacting with the orphan's wealth is **NOT permissible**?
   A. investing it in risky investments
   B. protecting it carefully
   C. increasing it with wise investments
   D. giving it to him entirely, once he is deemed to be responsible and mature

10. What rational argument does Allah provide in *Soorah al-Israa'* for those who claim that He actually has partners who are worthy of worship?
    A. If that were true, the sky would collapse.
    B. If that were true, they would all have sent prophets and messengers.
    C. Worship directed to them would ultimately reach Allah anyway.
    D. Had that been the case, such deities would have sought nearness to Allah.

11. What does Allah mention as the result of the pagans claiming that Muslims only follow a man who had magic spells put on him?
    A. They will be made to wear garments of iron in the Hellfire.
    B. They are lost and cannot find any path of guidance.
    C. Curses will be put on them in this life and in the Hereafter.
    D. Their idols will be incapable of protecting them from magic spells.

12. What is the event or time being asked about in the Verse [which means]: **"They will shake their heads at you and say, 'When will THAT be?'"**
    A. the return of 'Eesaa (Jesus), the son of Mary
    B. the Day of Judgment
    C. the conquering of Makkah
    D. the downfall of Rome

13. Allah says [what means]: *"And say to My slaves that they must say [only] what is best..."* Which of the following did al-Imam as-Sa'dee mention as a specific example of this?

    A. ordering good
    B. forbidding evil
    C. remembrance (*thikr*)
    D. all of the above

14. How did al-Imam as-Sa'dee explain Allah's Statement [which means], *"And We have not sent you (Muhammad) as a wakeel (guardian) over them..."*?

    A. You are not to advise them; you are only to command them.
    B. You are a *wakeel* over them, but We did not send you for this purpose.
    C. You are only someone who conveys a message and guides.
    D. all of the above

15. Allah negated that false deities can remove harm from their worshippers, nor can they "shift" that harm. What did al-Imam as-Sa'dee explain this "shift" to mean?

    A. shifting it from one geographical location to another
    B. shifting it from one person to another
    C. shifting it from one time period to another
    D. none of the above

16. Al-Imam as-Sa'dee mentioned that the sign of someone truly loving Allah is:

    A. exerting oneself in sincere acts of worship
    B. advising people to offer sincere worship
    C. both A and B
    D. neither A nor B

17. How did al-Imam as-Sa'dee explain that Iblees was granted permission to *"Share with them (humans) in wealth and children,"* as mentioned in the 64th Verse?

    A. mutilating livestock
    B. male Jinn having intercourse with some human women
    C. wearing gold and silk (for men)
    D. none of the above

18. Which of the following did al-Imam as-Sa'dee mention among his examples of how Allah has favored the children of Adam, in explanation of the 70th Verse?

    A. intellect
    B. knowledge
    C. both A and B
    D. neither A nor B

19. Allah says [what means], *"Indeed, they plotted to expel you from the land."* How did al-Imam as-Sa'dee explain this Verse?

    A. The pagans of Makkah plotted to expel the believers from al-Madeenah.
    B. The pagans of Makkah actually expelled the believers from Makkah
    C. The Jews of al-Madeenah were unable to expel the believers from al-Madeenah.
    D. The Jews of al-Madeenah actually expelled the believers from al-Madeenah.

20. What is the **"maqaam mahmood"** which our Prophet (صلى الله عليه وسلم) was encouraged to strive for, as explained by al-Imam as-Sa'dee?

    A. being admired in general, by Muslims and non-Muslims alike
    B. interceding for Aboo Taalib
    C. his *howdh* (pool) on the Day of Judgment
    D. none of the above

21. Al-Imam as-Sa'dee explained that the "healing" of the Quran is:

    A. exclusive to illnesses of the heart
    B. exclusive to weakness in faith
    C. applicable to illnesses of both the heart and the body
    D. only for physical illnesses of the body

22. When the people asked our Prophet (صلى الله عليه وسلم) about the *"rooh,"* Allah revealed:

    A. That the *"rooh"* is actually Jibreel.
    B. That the *"rooh"* is from the matters known to Allah
    C. That knowledge of the *"rooh"* is not beneficial.
    D. none of the above

23. Al-Imam as-Sa'dee extracted which of the following educational techniques from the question about the *"rooh"* and the answer provided by Allah?

    A. only teaching religious matters which are asked about, when they are asked
    B. shifting the focus of questioners to what is more beneficial for them
    C. answering religious questions while mounted on transportation
    D. ignoring some questions randomly

24. Allah exposes that if the disbelievers possessed the treasures of Allah's Mercy:

    A. Then, and only then, would they become dignified.
    B. They would be the most generous of the people.
    C. They would spend on themselves lavishly.
    D. none of the above

25. When did al-Imam as-Sa'dee complete his explanation of *Soorah al-Israa'*?

    A. the 7th day of Jumaadaa al-Oolaa, 1344
    B. the 1st day of Ramadhaan, 1310
    C. the 5th day of Rajab, 1381
    D. the 30th day of Ramadhaan, 1444

ANSWER KEY:

	QUIZ 1	QUIZ 2	QUIZ 3	QUIZ 4	QUIZ 5
1.	A	C	B	A	B
2.	D	A	D	B	D
3.	C	A	C	A	B
4.	A	D	A	C	B
5.	B	C	A	D	D
6.	A	B	B	C	C
7.	D	A	C	D	B
8.	A	B	A	B	C
9.	B	C	C	A	B
10.	B	D	A	D	D
11.				B	C
12.				D	B
13.				D	B
14.				C	D
15.				B	A

21. C
22. B
23. B
24. D
25. A

APPENDIX I: SOORAH AL-ISRAA'
AND A TRANSLATION OF ITS MEANINGS

*In the Name of Allah,
the Most Gracious, the Ever Merciful*

بِسْمِ ٱللَّهِ ٱلرَّحْمَٰنِ ٱلرَّحِيمِ

1. Exalted is He (Allah) Who took His slave for a journey by night from the sacred masjid (in Makkah) to the farthest masjid (in Jerusalem), which We had blessed all its surrounding areas, in order that We might show him some of Our Aayaat (proofs, evidences, signs, etc.). Verily, it is He (Allah) [Alone] Who is the All-Hearing, the All-Seeing.

سُبْحَٰنَ ٱلَّذِىٓ أَسْرَىٰ بِعَبْدِهِۦ لَيْلًا مِّنَ ٱلْمَسْجِدِ ٱلْحَرَامِ إِلَى ٱلْمَسْجِدِ ٱلْأَقْصَا ٱلَّذِى بَٰرَكْنَا حَوْلَهُۥ لِنُرِيَهُۥ مِنْ ءَايَٰتِنَآ ۚ إِنَّهُۥ هُوَ ٱلسَّمِيعُ ٱلْبَصِيرُ ۝

2. We had given Moosaa (Moses) the Book and made it guidance for the Children of Israel (saying): "Do not take other than Me as a protecting ally.

وَءَاتَيْنَا مُوسَى ٱلْكِتَٰبَ وَجَعَلْنَٰهُ هُدًى لِّبَنِىٓ إِسْرَٰٓءِيلَ أَلَّا تَتَّخِذُوا۟ مِن دُونِى وَكِيلًا ۝

3. O descendants of those whom We carried [in the ship] along with Nooh (Noah)! Verily, he was a grateful slave."

ذُرِّيَّةَ مَنْ حَمَلْنَا مَعَ نُوحٍ ۚ إِنَّهُۥ كَانَ عَبْدًا شَكُورًا ۝

4. We decreed for the Children of Israel in the Book, that you would in fact cause corruption on earth twice, and that you would actually become tyrants and extremely arrogant!

وَقَضَيْنَآ إِلَىٰ بَنِىٓ إِسْرَٰٓءِيلَ فِى ٱلْكِتَٰبِ لَتُفْسِدُنَّ فِى ٱلْأَرْضِ مَرَّتَيْنِ وَلَتَعْلُنَّ عُلُوًّا كَبِيرًا ۝

5. So when the set time came for the first of the two [decrees], We sent against you slaves of Ours, possessors of tremendous strength and might. They entered the very innermost parts of your homes; that was a promised event, fully enacted.

فَإِذَا جَآءَ وَعْدُ أُولَىٰهُمَا بَعَثْنَا عَلَيْكُمْ عِبَادًا لَّنَآ أُو۟لِى بَأْسٍ شَدِيدٍ فَجَاسُوا۟ خِلَٰلَ ٱلدِّيَارِ ۚ وَكَانَ وَعْدًا مَّفْعُولًا ۝

6. After that, We granted you a return of victory against them. We provided you with wealth and children, and We made you more in number than them.

ثُمَّ رَدَدْنَا لَكُمُ ٱلْكَرَّةَ عَلَيْهِمْ وَأَمْدَدْنَٰكُم بِأَمْوَٰلٍ وَبَنِينَ وَجَعَلْنَٰكُمْ أَكْثَرَ نَفِيرًا ۝

7. If you did things well, you did them well for your own souls. If you did evil, it was only against them (i.e. your souls). When the final (second) appointed time came to pass, it was to make your faces sorrowful, and for them (your enemies) to enter the masjid (of Jerusalem) as they had entered it before, and to destroy with utter destruction all places they gained authority over.

إِنْ أَحْسَنتُمْ أَحْسَنتُمْ لِأَنفُسِكُمْ ۖ وَإِنْ أَسَأْتُمْ فَلَهَا ۚ فَإِذَا جَآءَ وَعْدُ ٱلْءَاخِرَةِ لِيَسُۥٓـُٔوا۟ وُجُوهَكُمْ وَلِيَدْخُلُوا۟ ٱلْمَسْجِدَ كَمَا دَخَلُوهُ أَوَّلَ مَرَّةٍ وَلِيُتَبِّرُوا۟ مَا عَلَوْا۟ تَتْبِيرًا ۝

8. Perhaps your Lord may have Mercy on you, but if you return [to disobedience], We shall return [to punishing you]. And We made Hell to be a prison for the disbelievers.

9. Verily, this Quran guides to what is upright and gives glad tidings to the believers who work deeds of righteousness, that they shall have a great reward.

10. And [it warns that] those who do not believe in the Hereafter, for them We have prepared a painful torment.

11. Mankind supplicates for evil similar to how he supplicates for good; mankind is ever so hasty.

12. And We have made the night and the day to be two signs. We then wiped away [the light from] the sign of night, while We made the sign of day illuminating, so that you could seek bounty from your Lord, and so that you could know the number of years and [other] calculated matters. And We have explained everything in detail, with full explanation.

13. For every person, We have fastened his deeds to his neck, and on the Day of Judgment, We bring forth unto him a book which he finds wide open.

14. "Read your book. You yourself are sufficient as a reckoner against you on this Day."

15. Whoever followed guidance, it is only for the benefit of his own soul. Whoever went astray, he only goes astray at his own expense. No one shall bear the burden of another, and We never punish [anyone] until We first send a messenger.

16. Whenever We want to destroy a village, We first decree that the extravagant ones among them shall disobey therein, thus the verdict [of punishment] is justified against it (the village). Then We destroy it with complete destruction.

17. And how many previous generations did We destroy after Nooh (Noah)! Sufficient is your Lord as One who is All-Knowing and All-Seeing, regarding the sins of His slaves.

18. Whoever wishes for what is quick and temporary (i.e. the enjoyment of this worldly life), We bring that forth quickly for him, whatever We want of it for him. Yet, afterwards, We have prepared *Jahannam* for him, to enter it in disgrace and humiliation.

19. Yet whoever desires the Hereafter and strives for it, with the effort appropriate for it, while being a believer, such are the ones whose striving shall be appreciated.

20. To all, these and those alike, We extend for them from the bounties of your Lord, and the bounties of your Lord are never forbidden.

21. Consider how We favor some of them over others [in this worldly life], while the Hereafter is indeed a place of greater degrees [of reward] and even more favoring [of some over others].

22. Do not set up, along with Allah, any other deity, lest you end up humiliated and forsaken [in Hell].

23. Your Lord has decreed that you shall not worship anyone other than Him, and that you must be dutiful to parents. If one or both of them reach old age in your life, do not say to them, "Uff," (the slightest show of disrespect), nor rebuke them. Instead, only speak to them with a kind word.

24. And lower unto them the wing of humility, out of mercy, and say: "My Lord! Have Mercy on them, as they took care of me when I was young."

25. Your Lord knows best about what is within your souls. If you are righteous, then He is indeed Forgiving to those who continually and dutifully repent [to Him].

26. And give the close relative his right, and to the poor man and the traveler as well, but do not overspend wastefully.

27. Verily, spendthrifts are the brothers of the devils, and the devil is ever ungrateful to his Lord.

28. If you turn away from them [for now], anticipating Mercy from your Lord which you hope for [to give to them later], then speak to them a gentle word.

مَّن كَانَ يُرِيدُ ٱلْعَاجِلَةَ عَجَّلْنَا لَهُۥ فِيهَا مَا نَشَآءُ لِمَن نُّرِيدُ ثُمَّ جَعَلْنَا لَهُۥ جَهَنَّمَ يَصْلَىٰهَا مَذْمُومًا مَّدْحُورًا ۝

وَمَنْ أَرَادَ ٱلْءَاخِرَةَ وَسَعَىٰ لَهَا سَعْيَهَا وَهُوَ مُؤْمِنٌ فَأُو۟لَـٰٓئِكَ كَانَ سَعْيُهُم مَّشْكُورًا ۝

كُلًّا نُّمِدُّ هَـٰٓؤُلَآءِ وَهَـٰٓؤُلَآءِ مِنْ عَطَآءِ رَبِّكَ وَمَا كَانَ عَطَآءُ رَبِّكَ مَحْظُورًا ۝

ٱنظُرْ كَيْفَ فَضَّلْنَا بَعْضَهُمْ عَلَىٰ بَعْضٍ وَلَلْءَاخِرَةُ أَكْبَرُ دَرَجَـٰتٍ وَأَكْبَرُ تَفْضِيلًا ۝

لَّا تَجْعَلْ مَعَ ٱللَّهِ إِلَـٰهًا ءَاخَرَ فَتَقْعُدَ مَذْمُومًا مَّخْذُولًا ۝

وَقَضَىٰ رَبُّكَ أَلَّا تَعْبُدُوٓا۟ إِلَّآ إِيَّاهُ وَبِٱلْوَٰلِدَيْنِ إِحْسَـٰنًا إِمَّا يَبْلُغَنَّ عِندَكَ ٱلْكِبَرَ أَحَدُهُمَآ أَوْ كِلَاهُمَا فَلَا تَقُل لَّهُمَآ أُفٍّ وَلَا تَنْهَرْهُمَا وَقُل لَّهُمَا قَوْلًا كَرِيمًا ۝

وَٱخْفِضْ لَهُمَا جَنَاحَ ٱلذُّلِّ مِنَ ٱلرَّحْمَةِ وَقُل رَّبِّ ٱرْحَمْهُمَا كَمَا رَبَّيَانِى صَغِيرًا ۝

رَّبُّكُمْ أَعْلَمُ بِمَا فِى نُفُوسِكُمْ إِن تَكُونُوا۟ صَـٰلِحِينَ فَإِنَّهُۥ كَانَ لِلْأَوَّٰبِينَ غَفُورًا ۝

وَءَاتِ ذَا ٱلْقُرْبَىٰ حَقَّهُۥ وَٱلْمِسْكِينَ وَٱبْنَ ٱلسَّبِيلِ وَلَا تُبَذِّرْ تَبْذِيرًا ۝

إِنَّ ٱلْمُبَذِّرِينَ كَانُوٓا۟ إِخْوَٰنَ ٱلشَّيَـٰطِينِ وَكَانَ ٱلشَّيْطَـٰنُ لِرَبِّهِۦ كَفُورًا ۝

وَإِمَّا تُعْرِضَنَّ عَنْهُمُ ٱبْتِغَآءَ رَحْمَةٍ مِّن رَّبِّكَ تَرْجُوهَا فَقُل لَّهُمْ قَوْلًا مَّيْسُورًا ۝

29. Do not let your hand be tied up to your neck [in miserliness], nor stretch it forth to its utmost reach [wastefully], lest you end up blameworthy and impoverished.

30. Truly, your Lord grants abundant provisions to whomever He wills and limits that [for others]. Verily, regarding His slaves, He is All-Knowing and All-Seeing.

31. Do not kill not your children in fear of poverty. We provide for them and for you. Surely, killing them is a great sin.

32. And do not come anywhere close to unlawful sexual intercourse. Verily, that is a sinful obscenity, and what an evil path it is!

33. Also, do not take any life which Allah has forbidden, except by legitimate right. Whoever is oppressively killed, We have certainly granted his heir authority [to request the death penalty or demand blood money through Islamic courts]. Yet he must not transgress limits in [seeking] the death penalty. Verily, he is one who is aided [by Allah and through His Legislation].

34. And do not come anywhere near the orphan's property, except in ways that are best (i.e. good investments), until he attains his age of full strength. And fulfil (every) covenant; verily, the covenants will be asked about.

35. Give full portions when you measure [your goods], and weigh [them] with fair, precise balance. That is better and finer in consequence.

36. And do not follow after what you have no knowledge of. Verily, the hearing, the sight, and the heart, all of that will be asked about.

37. And do not walk about in the land arrogantly. Verily, you cannot crack the earth, nor could you reach a stature like the mountains in height.

38. All the bad aspects of these matters are hated by your Lord.

39. That is from the wisdom which your Lord has revealed to you. And do not set up any other deity in your worship of Allah, lest you be cast down into *Jahannam*, blameworthy and rejected.

88

40. Has then your Lord favored you [by providing you] with sons, while He takes Angels for Himself, as female offspring? Verily, you utter such a terrible claim, indeed.

41. And surely, We have provided [many rulings and lessons] in this Quran, in order for them to take heed, yet it only increases them in aversion [to the Truth].

42. Say: "Had there been other deities [worthy of worship] along with Him as they claim, they would certainly have sought nearness to the Owner of the Throne.

43. Exalted and Lofty He is, far above what they claim!"

44. The seven heavens and the earth and all that is within them exalt Him. There is not a thing which does not glorify Him in praise, yet you do not comprehend their exaltations. Truly, He is Ever Forbearing, Oft-Forgiving.

45. And when you recite the Quran, We place a hidden barrier between you and those who do not believe in the Hereafter.

46. And We place coverings over their hearts, preventing them from understanding it, and in their ears deafness. Whenever you mention your Lord Alone in the Quran, they turn their backs, fleeing [in contempt].

47. We know best of what they listen to, when they listen to you, and when they take secret counsel, as the oppressive ones say: "You follow nothing but a bewitched man."

48. Consider the kinds of likenesses they attribute to you, while they go astray and are unable to find any path [of guidance].

49. And they say: "When we are bones and scattered fragments, how could we really be resurrected as a new creation?"

أَفَأَصْفَىٰكُمْ رَبُّكُم بِٱلْبَنِينَ وَٱتَّخَذَ مِنَ ٱلْمَلَـٰٓئِكَةِ إِنَـٰثًا إِنَّكُمْ لَتَقُولُونَ قَوْلًا عَظِيمًا ﴿٤٠﴾

وَلَقَدْ صَرَّفْنَا فِى هَـٰذَا ٱلْقُرْءَانِ لِيَذَّكَّرُوا۟ وَمَا يَزِيدُهُمْ إِلَّا نُفُورًا ﴿٤١﴾

قُل لَّوْ كَانَ مَعَهُۥٓ ءَالِهَةٌ كَمَا يَقُولُونَ إِذًا لَّٱبْتَغَوْا۟ إِلَىٰ ذِى ٱلْعَرْشِ سَبِيلًا ﴿٤٢﴾

سُبْحَـٰنَهُۥ وَتَعَـٰلَىٰ عَمَّا يَقُولُونَ عُلُوًّا كَبِيرًا ﴿٤٣﴾

تُسَبِّحُ لَهُ ٱلسَّمَـٰوَٰتُ ٱلسَّبْعُ وَٱلْأَرْضُ وَمَن فِيهِنَّ وَإِن مِّن شَىْءٍ إِلَّا يُسَبِّحُ بِحَمْدِهِۦ وَلَـٰكِن لَّا تَفْقَهُونَ تَسْبِيحَهُمْ إِنَّهُۥ كَانَ حَلِيمًا غَفُورًا ﴿٤٤﴾

وَإِذَا قَرَأْتَ ٱلْقُرْءَانَ جَعَلْنَا بَيْنَكَ وَبَيْنَ ٱلَّذِينَ لَا يُؤْمِنُونَ بِٱلْـَٔاخِرَةِ حِجَابًا مَّسْتُورًا ﴿٤٥﴾

وَجَعَلْنَا عَلَىٰ قُلُوبِهِمْ أَكِنَّةً أَن يَفْقَهُوهُ وَفِىٓ ءَاذَانِهِمْ وَقْرًا وَإِذَا ذَكَرْتَ رَبَّكَ فِى ٱلْقُرْءَانِ وَحْدَهُۥ وَلَّوْا۟ عَلَىٰٓ أَدْبَـٰرِهِمْ نُفُورًا ﴿٤٦﴾

نَّحْنُ أَعْلَمُ بِمَا يَسْتَمِعُونَ بِهِۦٓ إِذْ يَسْتَمِعُونَ إِلَيْكَ وَإِذْ هُمْ نَجْوَىٰٓ إِذْ يَقُولُ ٱلظَّـٰلِمُونَ إِن تَتَّبِعُونَ إِلَّا رَجُلًا مَّسْحُورًا ﴿٤٧﴾

ٱنظُرْ كَيْفَ ضَرَبُوا۟ لَكَ ٱلْأَمْثَالَ فَضَلُّوا۟ فَلَا يَسْتَطِيعُونَ سَبِيلًا ﴿٤٨﴾

وَقَالُوٓا۟ أَءِذَا كُنَّا عِظَـٰمًا وَرُفَـٰتًا أَءِنَّا لَمَبْعُوثُونَ خَلْقًا جَدِيدًا ﴿٤٩﴾

50. Say: "Be you [objects made of] stones or iron,

51. Or some other created thing that is even greater in your breasts!" They will say: "Who could bring us back [to life]?" Say: "The One Who created you the first time!" Then, they will shake their heads at you [in disbelief] and say: "When will that be?" Say: "Perhaps it may be soon!"

52. On the Day when He calls you forth, and you respond with His praises. You will think that you have remained [in this worldly life] for only a short time.

53. And say to My slaves that they must say [only] what is best, since the devil surely causes enmity between them. Indeed, the devil is a plain enemy to mankind.

54. Your Lord knows you best. If He wills, He will have mercy on you; if He wills, He will punish you. And We have not sent you (Muhammad) as a guardian over them.

55. And your Lord knows best about all who are in the heavens and on earth. We have surely preferred some prophets over others; to Daawood (David) We gave the Zaboor (Psalms).

56. Say: "Call upon those besides Him whom you assume [to be worthy of worship]. They do not possess any power to remove adversity from you, or even to shift it in any way."

57. Those [objects of worship] whom they call upon are themselves seeking out ways to draw near to their Lord, hoping to be the closest [to Allah]. They hope for His Mercy and fear His Punishment. Verily, the Punishment of your Lord is ever something to be warned of!

58. And there is not a single village, except that We shall destroy it before the Day of Judgment, or punish it with a severe punishment. That is something written in the Book.

59. And nothing prevents Us from sending *Aayaat* (proofs, evidences, signs, etc.), but that the people of old rejected them. We sent the she-camel to Thamood, as [a thing providing] insight and understanding, but they oppressed, by way of her. And We only sent the *Aayaat* (proofs, signs, etc.) as warnings to be feared.

60. And [remember] when We told you: "Verily! Your Lord has encompassed the people (i.e. there is nowhere to flee from Him)." And We only made the vision we showed you (Muhammad) as a trial for mankind, and likewise the cursed tree [*az-Zaqqoom*, as mentioned] in the Quran. We make them afraid, yet it only increases them in serious transgressions.

61. And [remember] when We said to the angels, "Prostrate to Adam." They all prostrated, but Iblees (the devil) did not. He said, "Shall I prostrate to someone You created from clay?"

62. He said, "Do you see this one whom You have honored more than me? If You allow me respite until the Day of Judgment, I will surely lead his offspring astray, all but a few!"

63. He (Allah) said: "Go then, and whoever of them follows you, then *Jahannam* will be your recompense, an ample compensation.

64. "Trick those of them you can trick with your voice, attack them with your cavalry and infantry, mutually share with them in wealth and children, and make them promises." Yet, the devil promises them nothing but deceit.

65. "Verily, My [true] slaves, you shall have no authority over them. And All-Sufficient is your Lord as a Guardian."

66. Your Lord is the One Who enables the ship for you to sail through the sea, so that you might seek of His Bounty. Indeed, He is Ever Merciful to you all.

67. Whenever harm threatens you at sea, all those you call upon stray from you (i.e. you do not call upon any of them), except Him (Allah Alone). Yet, when He brings you safely to land, you turn away [from Him]. Mankind is ever so ungrateful!

91

68. Do you feel so secure that He would not cause a part of the land to swallow you up, or that He would not unleash upon you a violent sandstorm? You would then find no protector for yourselves!

69. Or do you feel so secure that He would not send you back a second time there [to the sea], and unleash upon you a hurricane of wind and drown you because of your disbelief? You would then not find any recourse against Us!

70. Indeed, We have truly honored the Children of Adam, and We have carried them on land and at sea. We have provided them with good, wholesome things, and We have preferred them over many of those whom We created, with distinguishing preference.

71. (Remember) the Day when We shall call forth all people along with their (respective) *imam* (i.e. leader, or book). Whoever is given his book in his right hand, such people shall read their books, and they will not be dealt with unjustly in the least.

72. And whoever is blind [to belief] in this world, such will be blind in the Hereafter, and even more astray.

73. Indeed, they plotted to divert you away from that which We have revealed to you (Muhammad), to fabricate something else from Us. They would certainly have taken you as a close friend [had they accomplished that]!

74. And had We not made you stand firm, you might have inclined towards them a little.

75. In that case, We would have made you taste a double portion [of punishment] in this life, as well as a double portion after dying. And then you would have found no one to help you against Us.

76. Indeed, they plotted to expel you from the land. In such a case, they would not remain after you, except for a little while.

77. [Such is] the Sunnah (way) of how We sent Our messengers before you (Muhammad); you will not find any change in Our Sunnah.

78. Establish prayer once the sun passes its zenith [at mid-day], until the darkness of night, and then [recite] the Quran at dawn! Verily, [the recitation of] the Quran at dawn is ever witnessed!

79. At some parts of the night offer optional prayers, additional [rewards] for you (Muhammad); perhaps your Lord will send you forth to a praiseworthy station [of Intercession].

80. And say: "My Lord! Grant me an entry of honesty and an exit of honesty, and give me from Yourself a victory of aid and support (through proofs and evidences)."

81. And say: "The Truth has come, and falsehood has vanished. Surely, falsehood is ever fading away."

82. And We send down among the Quran that which is a healing and a mercy to the believers, yet it does not increase the oppressive ones in anything but loss.

83. And whenever We bestow Our Grace on a [disbelieving] man, he arrogantly turns away, far away from the right path. Then, when evil reaches him he is ever in despair.

84. Say: "Each person behaves in line with his kind, and your Lord [Alone] knows best who is most guided to the right path."

85. And they ask you about the rooh (the spirit or soul). Say: "The rooh is among the matters for my Lord [to know and potentially reveal information about]. And of knowledge, you (mankind) have only been given a little."

86. And had We so willed, We could have done away with what We had revealed to you. Then you would have found no protector for yourself against Us.

87. Except as a Mercy from your Lord. Verily, His Favor upon you is ever great!

88. Say: "If mankind and the Jinn came together to bring about the likes of this Quran, they could not produce its likes, even if they all supported one another."

أَقِمِ ٱلصَّلَوٰةَ لِدُلُوكِ ٱلشَّمْسِ إِلَىٰ غَسَقِ ٱلَّيْلِ وَقُرْءَانَ ٱلْفَجْرِ إِنَّ قُرْءَانَ ٱلْفَجْرِ كَانَ مَشْهُودًا ۝

وَمِنَ ٱلَّيْلِ فَتَهَجَّدْ بِهِۦ نَافِلَةً لَّكَ عَسَىٰٓ أَن يَبْعَثَكَ رَبُّكَ مَقَامًا مَّحْمُودًا ۝

وَقُل رَّبِّ أَدْخِلْنِي مُدْخَلَ صِدْقٍ وَأَخْرِجْنِي مُخْرَجَ صِدْقٍ وَٱجْعَل لِّي مِن لَّدُنكَ سُلْطَٰنًا نَّصِيرًا ۝

وَقُلْ جَآءَ ٱلْحَقُّ وَزَهَقَ ٱلْبَٰطِلُ إِنَّ ٱلْبَٰطِلَ كَانَ زَهُوقًا ۝

وَنُنَزِّلُ مِنَ ٱلْقُرْءَانِ مَا هُوَ شِفَآءٌ وَرَحْمَةٌ لِّلْمُؤْمِنِينَ وَلَا يَزِيدُ ٱلظَّٰلِمِينَ إِلَّا خَسَارًا ۝

وَإِذَآ أَنْعَمْنَا عَلَى ٱلْإِنسَٰنِ أَعْرَضَ وَنَـَٔا بِجَانِبِهِۦ وَإِذَا مَسَّهُ ٱلشَّرُّ كَانَ يَـُٔوسًا ۝

قُلْ كُلٌّ يَعْمَلُ عَلَىٰ شَاكِلَتِهِۦ فَرَبُّكُمْ أَعْلَمُ بِمَنْ هُوَ أَهْدَىٰ سَبِيلًا ۝

وَيَسْـَٔلُونَكَ عَنِ ٱلرُّوحِ قُلِ ٱلرُّوحُ مِنْ أَمْرِ رَبِّي وَمَآ أُوتِيتُم مِّنَ ٱلْعِلْمِ إِلَّا قَلِيلًا ۝

وَلَئِن شِئْنَا لَنَذْهَبَنَّ بِٱلَّذِىٓ أَوْحَيْنَآ إِلَيْكَ ثُمَّ لَا تَجِدُ لَكَ بِهِۦ عَلَيْنَا وَكِيلًا ۝

إِلَّا رَحْمَةً مِّن رَّبِّكَ إِنَّ فَضْلَهُۥ كَانَ عَلَيْكَ كَبِيرًا ۝

قُل لَّئِنِ ٱجْتَمَعَتِ ٱلْإِنسُ وَٱلْجِنُّ عَلَىٰٓ أَن يَأْتُوا۟ بِمِثْلِ هَٰذَا ٱلْقُرْءَانِ لَا يَأْتُونَ بِمِثْلِهِۦ وَلَوْ كَانَ بَعْضُهُمْ لِبَعْضٍ ظَهِيرًا ۝

89. Indeed, We have fully explained to mankind in this Quran every type of similitude, yet most people still refuse anything but disbelief.

90. And they have said, "We will not believe for you (Muhammad), until you cause a spring to gush forth from the earth for us;

91. Or you have a garden of date-palm trees and grapes, and you cause rivers to gush forth in their midst abundantly;

92. Or you cause the heavens to fall upon us in pieces, as you have claimed [might happen], or you bring Allah and the angels to us, face to face;

93. Or you have a house of adornments, or you ascend up into the sky! But we would still not believe in your ascension unless you brought down for us a Book to read ourselves." Say: "Exalted is my Lord! Am I anything but a man, [sent as] a messenger?"

94. And nothing ever prevented people from believing when guidance came to them, except that they said: "Has Allah sent a human being as a messenger?"

95. Say: "Had there been [only] angels walking about on earth in tranquility, We should certainly have sent down from the heavens an angel as a messenger for them."

96. Say: "Sufficient is Allah as a witness between me and you. Verily, He [Alone] is All-Knowing, All-Seeing, regarding His slaves."

97. Whomever Allah guides, it is he who is rightly guided. Whomever He sends astray, for such you will find no allies [to help him] other than Him, and We shall gather them together on the Day of Judgment on their faces, blind, deaf, and dumb. Their abode will be *Jahannam*; every time it abates, We increase its blazing flames upon them.

98. That is their recompense, because they disbelieved in Our *Aayaat* (proofs, verses, signs, etc.) and said, "How could it be that after we are bones and fragments, we would really then be resurrected, as a new creation?"

99. Can they not see that Allah, the One Who created the heavens and the earth, is fully capable of creating their likes? And He has decreed for them an appointed term, about which there is no doubt. Yet, the oppressive people refuse everything but disbelief.

100. Say: "If you possessed the treasures of my Lord's Mercy, you would certainly hold back from spending in fear [of losing it]! Mankind is ever so miserly!"

101. And indeed We gave Moosaa (Moses) nine clear signs. Ask the Children of Israel about when he came to them and Pharaoh said to him: "O Moosaa (Moses)! I think you are indeed bewitched."

102. He (Moosaa) said: "Surely, you know that these signs have been sent down by none other than Lord of the heavens and the earth as clear evidences, providing knowledge and insight! And so I think it is you, O Pharaoh, who is actually doomed to destruction!"

103. So he (Pharaoh) wanted to exile them (Moosaa and the Children of Israel) out of the land, but We drowned him (Pharaoh) instead, along with everyone with him.

104. And We said to the Children of Israel after him: "Dwell in the land now, and when the final promise comes, We shall bring you all together!"

105. With truth We sent it (the Quran) down, and with truth it has come down. And We have only sent you (Muhammad) as a bearer of glad tidings and a warner.

106. And [it is] a Quran which We have divided into parts, so that you (Muhammad) would recite it to the people over time. And We have sent it down in stages of revelation.

107. Say: "Believe in it (the Quran), or do not believe. Verily, those who were given knowledge before it, when it is recited to them, they fall down on their faces in prostration."

95

108. And they say: "Exalted is our Lord! The Promise of our Lord will be enacted."

109. And they fall down on their faces weeping, and it increases them in humility.

110. Say: "Call upon Allah, or call upon ar-Rahmaan (the Most Gracious). Whichever [name] you call upon Him with, to Him belong the most beautiful Names." And do not be too loud in your prayers, nor be too quiet in them; instead seek a middle course between those ways.

111. And say: "All praise is due to Allah [Alone], the One Who has not taken a son, nor does He have any partner in (His) Sovereignty, nor does He have any caretaker because of weakness." And declare His Greatness with pure declarations.

وَيَقُولُونَ سُبْحَٰنَ رَبِّنَآ إِن كَانَ وَعْدُ رَبِّنَا لَمَفْعُولًا ۝

وَيَخِرُّونَ لِلْأَذْقَانِ يَبْكُونَ وَيَزِيدُهُمْ خُشُوعًا ۩ ۝

قُلِ ٱدْعُوا۟ ٱللَّهَ أَوِ ٱدْعُوا۟ ٱلرَّحْمَٰنَ ۖ أَيًّا مَّا تَدْعُوا۟ فَلَهُ ٱلْأَسْمَآءُ ٱلْحُسْنَىٰ ۚ وَلَا تَجْهَرْ بِصَلَاتِكَ وَلَا تُخَافِتْ بِهَا وَٱبْتَغِ بَيْنَ ذَٰلِكَ سَبِيلًا ۝

وَقُلِ ٱلْحَمْدُ لِلَّهِ ٱلَّذِى لَمْ يَتَّخِذْ وَلَدًا وَلَمْ يَكُن لَّهُۥ شَرِيكٌ فِى ٱلْمُلْكِ وَلَمْ يَكُن لَّهُۥ وَلِىٌّ مِّنَ ٱلذُّلِّ ۖ وَكَبِّرْهُ تَكْبِيرًۢا ۝

وَبِٱلْحَقِّ أَنزَلْنَٰهُ وَبِٱلْحَقِّ نَزَلَ ۗ وَمَآ أَرْسَلْنَٰكَ إِلَّا مُبَشِّرًا وَنَذِيرًا ۝١٠٥ وَقُرْءَانًا فَرَقْنَٰهُ لِتَقْرَأَهُۥ عَلَى ٱلنَّاسِ عَلَىٰ مُكْثٍ وَنَزَّلْنَٰهُ تَنزِيلًا ۝١٠٦ قُلْ ءَامِنُوا۟ بِهِۦٓ أَوْ لَا تُؤْمِنُوٓا۟ ۚ إِنَّ ٱلَّذِينَ أُوتُوا۟ ٱلْعِلْمَ مِن قَبْلِهِۦٓ إِذَا يُتْلَىٰ عَلَيْهِمْ يَخِرُّونَ لِلْأَذْقَانِ سُجَّدًا ۝١٠٧ وَيَقُولُونَ سُبْحَٰنَ رَبِّنَآ إِن كَانَ وَعْدُ رَبِّنَا لَمَفْعُولًا ۝١٠٨ وَيَخِرُّونَ لِلْأَذْقَانِ يَبْكُونَ وَيَزِيدُهُمْ خُشُوعًا ۩ ۝١٠٩ قُلِ ٱدْعُوا۟ ٱللَّهَ أَوِ ٱدْعُوا۟ ٱلرَّحْمَٰنَ ۖ أَيًّا مَّا تَدْعُوا۟ فَلَهُ ٱلْأَسْمَآءُ ٱلْحُسْنَىٰ ۚ وَلَا تَجْهَرْ بِصَلَاتِكَ وَلَا تُخَافِتْ بِهَا وَٱبْتَغِ بَيْنَ ذَٰلِكَ سَبِيلًا ۝١١٠ وَقُلِ ٱلْحَمْدُ لِلَّهِ ٱلَّذِى لَمْ يَتَّخِذْ وَلَدًا وَلَمْ يَكُن لَّهُۥ شَرِيكٌ فِى ٱلْمُلْكِ وَلَمْ يَكُن لَّهُۥ وَلِىٌّ مِّنَ ٱلذُّلِّ ۖ وَكَبِّرْهُ تَكْبِيرًۢا ۝١١١

سُورَةُ الكَهْفِ

بِسْمِ ٱللَّهِ ٱلرَّحْمَٰنِ ٱلرَّحِيمِ

ٱلْحَمْدُ لِلَّهِ ٱلَّذِىٓ أَنزَلَ عَلَىٰ عَبْدِهِ ٱلْكِتَٰبَ وَلَمْ يَجْعَل لَّهُۥ عِوَجَا ۝١ قَيِّمًا لِّيُنذِرَ بَأْسًا شَدِيدًا مِّن لَّدُنْهُ وَيُبَشِّرَ ٱلْمُؤْمِنِينَ ٱلَّذِينَ يَعْمَلُونَ ٱلصَّٰلِحَٰتِ أَنَّ لَهُمْ أَجْرًا حَسَنًا ۝٢ مَّٰكِثِينَ فِيهِ أَبَدًا ۝٣ وَيُنذِرَ ٱلَّذِينَ قَالُوا۟ ٱتَّخَذَ ٱللَّهُ وَلَدًا ۝٤

وَمَن يَهْدِ ٱللَّهُ فَهُوَ ٱلْمُهْتَدِ ۖ وَمَن يُضْلِلْ فَلَن تَجِدَ لَهُمْ أَوْلِيَاءَ مِن دُونِهِۦ ۖ وَنَحْشُرُهُمْ يَوْمَ ٱلْقِيَٰمَةِ عَلَىٰ وُجُوهِهِمْ عُمْيًا وَبُكْمًا وَصُمًّا ۖ مَّأْوَىٰهُمْ جَهَنَّمُ ۖ كُلَّمَا خَبَتْ زِدْنَٰهُمْ سَعِيرًا ۝٩٧ ذَٰلِكَ جَزَآؤُهُم بِأَنَّهُمْ كَفَرُوا۟ بِـَٔايَٰتِنَا وَقَالُوٓا۟ أَءِذَا كُنَّا عِظَٰمًا وَرُفَٰتًا أَءِنَّا لَمَبْعُوثُونَ خَلْقًا جَدِيدًا ۝٩٨ ۞ أَوَلَمْ يَرَوْا۟ أَنَّ ٱللَّهَ ٱلَّذِى خَلَقَ ٱلسَّمَٰوَٰتِ وَٱلْأَرْضَ قَادِرٌ عَلَىٰٓ أَن يَخْلُقَ مِثْلَهُمْ وَجَعَلَ لَهُمْ أَجَلًا لَّا رَيْبَ فِيهِ فَأَبَى ٱلظَّٰلِمُونَ إِلَّا كُفُورًا ۝٩٩ قُل لَّوْ أَنتُمْ تَمْلِكُونَ خَزَآئِنَ رَحْمَةِ رَبِّىٓ إِذًا لَّأَمْسَكْتُمْ خَشْيَةَ ٱلْإِنفَاقِ ۚ وَكَانَ ٱلْإِنسَٰنُ قَتُورًا ۝١٠٠ وَلَقَدْ ءَاتَيْنَا مُوسَىٰ تِسْعَ ءَايَٰتٍۭ بَيِّنَٰتٍ ۖ فَسْـَٔلْ بَنِىٓ إِسْرَٰٓءِيلَ إِذْ جَآءَهُمْ فَقَالَ لَهُۥ فِرْعَوْنُ إِنِّى لَأَظُنُّكَ يَٰمُوسَىٰ مَسْحُورًا ۝١٠١ قَالَ لَقَدْ عَلِمْتَ مَآ أَنزَلَ هَٰٓؤُلَآءِ إِلَّا رَبُّ ٱلسَّمَٰوَٰتِ وَٱلْأَرْضِ بَصَآئِرَ وَإِنِّى لَأَظُنُّكَ يَٰفِرْعَوْنُ مَثْبُورًا ۝١٠٢ فَأَرَادَ أَن يَسْتَفِزَّهُم مِّنَ ٱلْأَرْضِ فَأَغْرَقْنَٰهُ وَمَن مَّعَهُۥ جَمِيعًا ۝١٠٣ وَقُلْنَا مِنۢ بَعْدِهِۦ لِبَنِىٓ إِسْرَٰٓءِيلَ ٱسْكُنُوا۟ ٱلْأَرْضَ فَإِذَا جَآءَ وَعْدُ ٱلْءَاخِرَةِ جِئْنَا بِكُمْ لَفِيفًا ۝١٠٤

إِلَّا رَحْمَةً مِّن رَّبِّكَ إِنَّ فَضْلَهُ كَانَ عَلَيْكَ كَبِيرًا ۝ قُل لَّئِنِ اجْتَمَعَتِ الْإِنسُ وَالْجِنُّ عَلَىٰ أَن يَأْتُوا بِمِثْلِ هَـٰذَا الْقُرْآنِ لَا يَأْتُونَ بِمِثْلِهِ وَلَوْ كَانَ بَعْضُهُمْ لِبَعْضٍ ظَهِيرًا ۝ وَلَقَدْ صَرَّفْنَا لِلنَّاسِ فِي هَـٰذَا الْقُرْآنِ مِن كُلِّ مَثَلٍ فَأَبَىٰ أَكْثَرُ النَّاسِ إِلَّا كُفُورًا ۝ وَقَالُوا لَن نُّؤْمِنَ لَكَ حَتَّىٰ تَفْجُرَ لَنَا مِنَ الْأَرْضِ يَنبُوعًا ۝ أَوْ تَكُونَ لَكَ جَنَّةٌ مِّن نَّخِيلٍ وَعِنَبٍ فَتُفَجِّرَ الْأَنْهَارَ خِلَالَهَا تَفْجِيرًا ۝ أَوْ تُسْقِطَ السَّمَاءَ كَمَا زَعَمْتَ عَلَيْنَا كِسَفًا أَوْ تَأْتِيَ بِاللَّهِ وَالْمَلَائِكَةِ قَبِيلًا ۝ أَوْ يَكُونَ لَكَ بَيْتٌ مِّن زُخْرُفٍ أَوْ تَرْقَىٰ فِي السَّمَاءِ وَلَن نُّؤْمِنَ لِرُقِيِّكَ حَتَّىٰ تُنَزِّلَ عَلَيْنَا كِتَابًا نَّقْرَؤُهُ ۗ قُلْ سُبْحَانَ رَبِّي هَلْ كُنتُ إِلَّا بَشَرًا رَّسُولًا ۝ وَمَا مَنَعَ النَّاسَ أَن يُؤْمِنُوا إِذْ جَاءَهُمُ الْهُدَىٰ إِلَّا أَن قَالُوا أَبَعَثَ اللَّهُ بَشَرًا رَّسُولًا ۝ قُل لَّوْ كَانَ فِي الْأَرْضِ مَلَائِكَةٌ يَمْشُونَ مُطْمَئِنِّينَ لَنَزَّلْنَا عَلَيْهِم مِّنَ السَّمَاءِ مَلَكًا رَّسُولًا ۝ قُلْ كَفَىٰ بِاللَّهِ شَهِيدًا بَيْنِي وَبَيْنَكُمْ ۚ إِنَّهُ كَانَ بِعِبَادِهِ خَبِيرًا بَصِيرًا ۝

٢٩١

وَإِن كَادُواْ لَيَسْتَفِزُّونَكَ مِنَ ٱلْأَرْضِ لِيُخْرِجُوكَ مِنْهَا ۖ وَإِذًا لَّا يَلْبَثُونَ خِلَافَكَ إِلَّا قَلِيلًا ۝ سُنَّةَ مَن قَدْ أَرْسَلْنَا قَبْلَكَ مِن رُّسُلِنَا ۖ وَلَا تَجِدُ لِسُنَّتِنَا تَحْوِيلًا ۝ أَقِمِ ٱلصَّلَوٰةَ لِدُلُوكِ ٱلشَّمْسِ إِلَىٰ غَسَقِ ٱلَّيْلِ وَقُرْءَانَ ٱلْفَجْرِ ۖ إِنَّ قُرْءَانَ ٱلْفَجْرِ كَانَ مَشْهُودًا ۝ وَمِنَ ٱلَّيْلِ فَتَهَجَّدْ بِهِۦ نَافِلَةً لَّكَ عَسَىٰٓ أَن يَبْعَثَكَ رَبُّكَ مَقَامًا مَّحْمُودًا ۝ وَقُل رَّبِّ أَدْخِلْنِى مُدْخَلَ صِدْقٍ وَأَخْرِجْنِى مُخْرَجَ صِدْقٍ وَٱجْعَل لِّى مِن لَّدُنكَ سُلْطَانًا نَّصِيرًا ۝ وَقُلْ جَآءَ ٱلْحَقُّ وَزَهَقَ ٱلْبَاطِلُ ۚ إِنَّ ٱلْبَاطِلَ كَانَ زَهُوقًا ۝ وَنُنَزِّلُ مِنَ ٱلْقُرْءَانِ مَا هُوَ شِفَآءٌ وَرَحْمَةٌ لِّلْمُؤْمِنِينَ ۙ وَلَا يَزِيدُ ٱلظَّٰلِمِينَ إِلَّا خَسَارًا ۝ وَإِذَآ أَنْعَمْنَا عَلَى ٱلْإِنسَانِ أَعْرَضَ وَنَـَٔا بِجَانِبِهِۦ ۖ وَإِذَا مَسَّهُ ٱلشَّرُّ كَانَ يَـُٔوسًا ۝ قُلْ كُلٌّ يَعْمَلُ عَلَىٰ شَاكِلَتِهِۦ فَرَبُّكُمْ أَعْلَمُ بِمَنْ هُوَ أَهْدَىٰ سَبِيلًا ۝ وَيَسْـَٔلُونَكَ عَنِ ٱلرُّوحِ ۖ قُلِ ٱلرُّوحُ مِنْ أَمْرِ رَبِّى وَمَآ أُوتِيتُم مِّنَ ٱلْعِلْمِ إِلَّا قَلِيلًا ۝ وَلَئِن شِئْنَا لَنَذْهَبَنَّ بِٱلَّذِىٓ أَوْحَيْنَآ إِلَيْكَ ثُمَّ لَا تَجِدُ لَكَ بِهِۦ عَلَيْنَا وَكِيلًا ۝

وَإِذَا مَسَّكُمُ ٱلضُّرُّ فِى ٱلْبَحْرِ ضَلَّ مَن تَدْعُونَ إِلَّآ إِيَّاهُ ۖ فَلَمَّا نَجَّىٰكُمْ إِلَى ٱلْبَرِّ أَعْرَضْتُمْ ۚ وَكَانَ ٱلْإِنسَٰنُ كَفُورًا ۝٦٧ أَفَأَمِنتُمْ أَن يَخْسِفَ بِكُمْ جَانِبَ ٱلْبَرِّ أَوْ يُرْسِلَ عَلَيْكُمْ حَاصِبًا ثُمَّ لَا تَجِدُوا۟ لَكُمْ وَكِيلًا ۝٦٨ أَمْ أَمِنتُمْ أَن يُعِيدَكُمْ فِيهِ تَارَةً أُخْرَىٰ فَيُرْسِلَ عَلَيْكُمْ قَاصِفًا مِّنَ ٱلرِّيحِ فَيُغْرِقَكُم بِمَا كَفَرْتُمْ ۙ ثُمَّ لَا تَجِدُوا۟ لَكُمْ عَلَيْنَا بِهِۦ تَبِيعًا ۝٦٩ ۞ وَلَقَدْ كَرَّمْنَا بَنِىٓ ءَادَمَ وَحَمَلْنَٰهُمْ فِى ٱلْبَرِّ وَٱلْبَحْرِ وَرَزَقْنَٰهُم مِّنَ ٱلطَّيِّبَٰتِ وَفَضَّلْنَٰهُمْ عَلَىٰ كَثِيرٍ مِّمَّنْ خَلَقْنَا تَفْضِيلًا ۝٧٠ يَوْمَ نَدْعُوا۟ كُلَّ أُنَاسٍۭ بِإِمَٰمِهِمْ ۖ فَمَنْ أُوتِىَ كِتَٰبَهُۥ بِيَمِينِهِۦ فَأُو۟لَٰٓئِكَ يَقْرَءُونَ كِتَٰبَهُمْ وَلَا يُظْلَمُونَ فَتِيلًا ۝٧١ وَمَن كَانَ فِى هَٰذِهِۦٓ أَعْمَىٰ فَهُوَ فِى ٱلْءَاخِرَةِ أَعْمَىٰ وَأَضَلُّ سَبِيلًا ۝٧٢ وَإِن كَادُوا۟ لَيَفْتِنُونَكَ عَنِ ٱلَّذِىٓ أَوْحَيْنَآ إِلَيْكَ لِتَفْتَرِىَ عَلَيْنَا غَيْرَهُۥ ۖ وَإِذًا لَّٱتَّخَذُوكَ خَلِيلًا ۝٧٣ وَلَوْلَآ أَن ثَبَّتْنَٰكَ لَقَدْ كِدتَّ تَرْكَنُ إِلَيْهِمْ شَيْـًٔا قَلِيلًا ۝٧٤ إِذًا لَّأَذَقْنَٰكَ ضِعْفَ ٱلْحَيَوٰةِ وَضِعْفَ ٱلْمَمَاتِ ثُمَّ لَا تَجِدُ لَكَ عَلَيْنَا نَصِيرًا ۝٧٥

وَمَا مَنَعَنَا أَن نُّرْسِلَ بِٱلْءَايَٰتِ إِلَّآ أَن كَذَّبَ بِهَا ٱلْأَوَّلُونَ ۚ وَءَاتَيْنَا ثَمُودَ ٱلنَّاقَةَ مُبْصِرَةً فَظَلَمُوا۟ بِهَا ۚ وَمَا نُرْسِلُ بِٱلْءَايَٰتِ إِلَّا تَخْوِيفًا ۝ وَإِذْ قُلْنَا لَكَ إِنَّ رَبَّكَ أَحَاطَ بِٱلنَّاسِ ۚ وَمَا جَعَلْنَا ٱلرُّءْيَا ٱلَّتِىٓ أَرَيْنَٰكَ إِلَّا فِتْنَةً لِّلنَّاسِ وَٱلشَّجَرَةَ ٱلْمَلْعُونَةَ فِى ٱلْقُرْءَانِ ۚ وَنُخَوِّفُهُمْ فَمَا يَزِيدُهُمْ إِلَّا طُغْيَٰنًا كَبِيرًا ۝ وَإِذْ قُلْنَا لِلْمَلَٰٓئِكَةِ ٱسْجُدُوا۟ لِءَادَمَ فَسَجَدُوٓا۟ إِلَّآ إِبْلِيسَ قَالَ ءَأَسْجُدُ لِمَنْ خَلَقْتَ طِينًا ۝ قَالَ أَرَءَيْتَكَ هَٰذَا ٱلَّذِى كَرَّمْتَ عَلَىَّ لَئِنْ أَخَّرْتَنِ إِلَىٰ يَوْمِ ٱلْقِيَٰمَةِ لَأَحْتَنِكَنَّ ذُرِّيَّتَهُۥٓ إِلَّا قَلِيلًا ۝ قَالَ ٱذْهَبْ فَمَن تَبِعَكَ مِنْهُمْ فَإِنَّ جَهَنَّمَ جَزَآؤُكُمْ جَزَآءً مَّوْفُورًا ۝ وَٱسْتَفْزِزْ مَنِ ٱسْتَطَعْتَ مِنْهُم بِصَوْتِكَ وَأَجْلِبْ عَلَيْهِم بِخَيْلِكَ وَرَجِلِكَ وَشَارِكْهُمْ فِى ٱلْأَمْوَٰلِ وَٱلْأَوْلَٰدِ وَعِدْهُمْ ۚ وَمَا يَعِدُهُمُ ٱلشَّيْطَٰنُ إِلَّا غُرُورًا ۝ إِنَّ عِبَادِى لَيْسَ لَكَ عَلَيْهِمْ سُلْطَٰنٌ ۚ وَكَفَىٰ بِرَبِّكَ وَكِيلًا ۝ رَّبُّكُمُ ٱلَّذِى يُزْجِى لَكُمُ ٱلْفُلْكَ فِى ٱلْبَحْرِ لِتَبْتَغُوا۟ مِن فَضْلِهِۦٓ ۚ إِنَّهُۥ كَانَ بِكُمْ رَحِيمًا ۝

سورة الإسراء

* قُلْ كُونُوا۟ حِجَارَةً أَوْ حَدِيدًا ۝ أَوْ خَلْقًا مِّمَّا يَكْبُرُ فِى صُدُورِكُمْ ۚ فَسَيَقُولُونَ مَن يُعِيدُنَا ۖ قُلِ ٱلَّذِى فَطَرَكُمْ أَوَّلَ مَرَّةٍ ۚ فَسَيُنْغِضُونَ إِلَيْكَ رُءُوسَهُمْ وَيَقُولُونَ مَتَىٰ هُوَ ۖ قُلْ عَسَىٰٓ أَن يَكُونَ قَرِيبًا ۝ يَوْمَ يَدْعُوكُمْ فَتَسْتَجِيبُونَ بِحَمْدِهِۦ وَتَظُنُّونَ إِن لَّبِثْتُمْ إِلَّا قَلِيلًا ۝ وَقُل لِّعِبَادِى يَقُولُوا۟ ٱلَّتِى هِىَ أَحْسَنُ ۚ إِنَّ ٱلشَّيْطَـٰنَ يَنزَغُ بَيْنَهُمْ ۚ إِنَّ ٱلشَّيْطَـٰنَ كَانَ لِلْإِنسَـٰنِ عَدُوًّا مُّبِينًا ۝ رَّبُّكُمْ أَعْلَمُ بِكُمْ ۖ إِن يَشَأْ يَرْحَمْكُمْ أَوْ إِن يَشَأْ يُعَذِّبْكُمْ ۚ وَمَآ أَرْسَلْنَـٰكَ عَلَيْهِمْ وَكِيلًا ۝ وَرَبُّكَ أَعْلَمُ بِمَن فِى ٱلسَّمَـٰوَٰتِ وَٱلْأَرْضِ ۗ وَلَقَدْ فَضَّلْنَا بَعْضَ ٱلنَّبِيِّـۦنَ عَلَىٰ بَعْضٍ ۖ وَءَاتَيْنَا دَاوُۥدَ زَبُورًا ۝ قُلِ ٱدْعُوا۟ ٱلَّذِينَ زَعَمْتُم مِّن دُونِهِۦ فَلَا يَمْلِكُونَ كَشْفَ ٱلضُّرِّ عَنكُمْ وَلَا تَحْوِيلًا ۝ أُو۟لَـٰٓئِكَ ٱلَّذِينَ يَدْعُونَ يَبْتَغُونَ إِلَىٰ رَبِّهِمُ ٱلْوَسِيلَةَ أَيُّهُمْ أَقْرَبُ وَيَرْجُونَ رَحْمَتَهُۥ وَيَخَافُونَ عَذَابَهُۥٓ ۚ إِنَّ عَذَابَ رَبِّكَ كَانَ مَحْذُورًا ۝ وَإِن مِّن قَرْيَةٍ إِلَّا نَحْنُ مُهْلِكُوهَا قَبْلَ يَوْمِ ٱلْقِيَـٰمَةِ أَوْ مُعَذِّبُوهَا عَذَابًا شَدِيدًا ۚ كَانَ ذَٰلِكَ فِى ٱلْكِتَـٰبِ مَسْطُورًا ۝

٢٨٧

ذَٰلِكَ مِمَّا أَوْحَىٰ إِلَيْكَ رَبُّكَ مِنَ ٱلْحِكْمَةِ وَلَا تَجْعَلْ مَعَ ٱللَّهِ إِلَٰهًا ءَاخَرَ فَتُلْقَىٰ فِي جَهَنَّمَ مَلُومًا مَّدْحُورًا ۝٣٩ أَفَأَصْفَىٰكُمْ رَبُّكُم بِٱلْبَنِينَ وَٱتَّخَذَ مِنَ ٱلْمَلَٰٓئِكَةِ إِنَٰثًا ۚ إِنَّكُمْ لَتَقُولُونَ قَوْلًا عَظِيمًا ۝٤٠ وَلَقَدْ صَرَّفْنَا فِي هَٰذَا ٱلْقُرْءَانِ لِيَذَّكَّرُوا۟ وَمَا يَزِيدُهُمْ إِلَّا نُفُورًا ۝٤١ قُل لَّوْ كَانَ مَعَهُۥٓ ءَالِهَةٌ كَمَا يَقُولُونَ إِذًا لَّٱبْتَغَوْا۟ إِلَىٰ ذِي ٱلْعَرْشِ سَبِيلًا ۝٤٢ سُبْحَٰنَهُۥ وَتَعَٰلَىٰ عَمَّا يَقُولُونَ عُلُوًّا كَبِيرًا ۝٤٣ تُسَبِّحُ لَهُ ٱلسَّمَٰوَٰتُ ٱلسَّبْعُ وَٱلْأَرْضُ وَمَن فِيهِنَّ ۚ وَإِن مِّن شَىْءٍ إِلَّا يُسَبِّحُ بِحَمْدِهِۦ وَلَٰكِن لَّا تَفْقَهُونَ تَسْبِيحَهُمْ ۗ إِنَّهُۥ كَانَ حَلِيمًا غَفُورًا ۝٤٤ وَإِذَا قَرَأْتَ ٱلْقُرْءَانَ جَعَلْنَا بَيْنَكَ وَبَيْنَ ٱلَّذِينَ لَا يُؤْمِنُونَ بِٱلْءَاخِرَةِ حِجَابًا مَّسْتُورًا ۝٤٥ وَجَعَلْنَا عَلَىٰ قُلُوبِهِمْ أَكِنَّةً أَن يَفْقَهُوهُ وَفِىٓ ءَاذَانِهِمْ وَقْرًا ۚ وَإِذَا ذَكَرْتَ رَبَّكَ فِي ٱلْقُرْءَانِ وَحْدَهُۥ وَلَّوْا۟ عَلَىٰٓ أَدْبَٰرِهِمْ نُفُورًا ۝٤٦ نَّحْنُ أَعْلَمُ بِمَا يَسْتَمِعُونَ بِهِۦٓ إِذْ يَسْتَمِعُونَ إِلَيْكَ وَإِذْ هُمْ نَجْوَىٰٓ إِذْ يَقُولُ ٱلظَّٰلِمُونَ إِن تَتَّبِعُونَ إِلَّا رَجُلًا مَّسْحُورًا ۝٤٧ ٱنظُرْ كَيْفَ ضَرَبُوا۟ لَكَ ٱلْأَمْثَالَ فَضَلُّوا۟ فَلَا يَسْتَطِيعُونَ سَبِيلًا ۝٤٨ وَقَالُوٓا۟ أَءِذَا كُنَّا عِظَٰمًا وَرُفَٰتًا أَءِنَّا لَمَبْعُوثُونَ خَلْقًا جَدِيدًا ۝٤٩

وَإِمَّا تُعْرِضَنَّ عَنْهُمُ ٱبْتِغَآءَ رَحْمَةٍ مِّن رَّبِّكَ تَرْجُوهَا فَقُل لَّهُمْ قَوْلًا مَّيْسُورًا ۝ وَلَا تَجْعَلْ يَدَكَ مَغْلُولَةً إِلَىٰ عُنُقِكَ وَلَا تَبْسُطْهَا كُلَّ ٱلْبَسْطِ فَتَقْعُدَ مَلُومًا مَّحْسُورًا ۝ إِنَّ رَبَّكَ يَبْسُطُ ٱلرِّزْقَ لِمَن يَشَآءُ وَيَقْدِرُ ۚ إِنَّهُۥ كَانَ بِعِبَادِهِۦ خَبِيرًۢا بَصِيرًا ۝ وَلَا تَقْتُلُوٓا۟ أَوْلَـٰدَكُمْ خَشْيَةَ إِمْلَـٰقٍ ۖ نَّحْنُ نَرْزُقُهُمْ وَإِيَّاكُمْ ۚ إِنَّ قَتْلَهُمْ كَانَ خِطْـًٔا كَبِيرًا ۝ وَلَا تَقْرَبُوا۟ ٱلزِّنَىٰٓ ۖ إِنَّهُۥ كَانَ فَـٰحِشَةً وَسَآءَ سَبِيلًا ۝ وَلَا تَقْتُلُوا۟ ٱلنَّفْسَ ٱلَّتِى حَرَّمَ ٱللَّهُ إِلَّا بِٱلْحَقِّ ۗ وَمَن قُتِلَ مَظْلُومًا فَقَدْ جَعَلْنَا لِوَلِيِّهِۦ سُلْطَـٰنًا فَلَا يُسْرِف فِّى ٱلْقَتْلِ ۖ إِنَّهُۥ كَانَ مَنصُورًا ۝ وَلَا تَقْرَبُوا۟ مَالَ ٱلْيَتِيمِ إِلَّا بِٱلَّتِى هِىَ أَحْسَنُ حَتَّىٰ يَبْلُغَ أَشُدَّهُۥ ۚ وَأَوْفُوا۟ بِٱلْعَهْدِ ۖ إِنَّ ٱلْعَهْدَ كَانَ مَسْـُٔولًا ۝ وَأَوْفُوا۟ ٱلْكَيْلَ إِذَا كِلْتُمْ وَزِنُوا۟ بِٱلْقِسْطَاسِ ٱلْمُسْتَقِيمِ ۚ ذَٰلِكَ خَيْرٌ وَأَحْسَنُ تَأْوِيلًا ۝ وَلَا تَقْفُ مَا لَيْسَ لَكَ بِهِۦ عِلْمٌ ۚ إِنَّ ٱلسَّمْعَ وَٱلْبَصَرَ وَٱلْفُؤَادَ كُلُّ أُو۟لَـٰٓئِكَ كَانَ عَنْهُ مَسْـُٔولًا ۝ وَلَا تَمْشِ فِى ٱلْأَرْضِ مَرَحًا ۖ إِنَّكَ لَن تَخْرِقَ ٱلْأَرْضَ وَلَن تَبْلُغَ ٱلْجِبَالَ طُولًا ۝ كُلُّ ذَٰلِكَ كَانَ سَيِّئُهُۥ عِندَ رَبِّكَ مَكْرُوهًا ۝

سُورَةُ الإِسْرَاءِ — الجزءُ الخامسَ عشرَ

مَن كَانَ يُرِيدُ ٱلْعَاجِلَةَ عَجَّلْنَا لَهُۥ فِيهَا مَا نَشَآءُ لِمَن نُّرِيدُ ثُمَّ جَعَلْنَا لَهُۥ جَهَنَّمَ يَصْلَىٰهَا مَذْمُومًا مَّدْحُورًا ۝١٨ وَمَنْ أَرَادَ ٱلْأَخِرَةَ وَسَعَىٰ لَهَا سَعْيَهَا وَهُوَ مُؤْمِنٌ فَأُو۟لَٰٓئِكَ كَانَ سَعْيُهُم مَّشْكُورًا ۝١٩ كُلًّا نُّمِدُّ هَٰٓؤُلَآءِ وَهَٰٓؤُلَآءِ مِنْ عَطَآءِ رَبِّكَ ۚ وَمَا كَانَ عَطَآءُ رَبِّكَ مَحْظُورًا ۝٢٠ ٱنظُرْ كَيْفَ فَضَّلْنَا بَعْضَهُمْ عَلَىٰ بَعْضٍ ۚ وَلَلْأَخِرَةُ أَكْبَرُ دَرَجَٰتٍ وَأَكْبَرُ تَفْضِيلًا ۝٢١ لَّا تَجْعَلْ مَعَ ٱللَّهِ إِلَٰهًا ءَاخَرَ فَتَقْعُدَ مَذْمُومًا مَّخْذُولًا ۝٢٢ ۞ وَقَضَىٰ رَبُّكَ أَلَّا تَعْبُدُوٓا۟ إِلَّآ إِيَّاهُ وَبِٱلْوَٰلِدَيْنِ إِحْسَٰنًا ۚ إِمَّا يَبْلُغَنَّ عِندَكَ ٱلْكِبَرَ أَحَدُهُمَآ أَوْ كِلَاهُمَا فَلَا تَقُل لَّهُمَآ أُفٍّ وَلَا تَنْهَرْهُمَا وَقُل لَّهُمَا قَوْلًا كَرِيمًا ۝٢٣ وَٱخْفِضْ لَهُمَا جَنَاحَ ٱلذُّلِّ مِنَ ٱلرَّحْمَةِ وَقُل رَّبِّ ٱرْحَمْهُمَا كَمَا رَبَّيَانِى صَغِيرًا ۝٢٤ رَّبُّكُمْ أَعْلَمُ بِمَا فِى نُفُوسِكُمْ ۚ إِن تَكُونُوا۟ صَٰلِحِينَ فَإِنَّهُۥ كَانَ لِلْأَوَّٰبِينَ غَفُورًا ۝٢٥ وَءَاتِ ذَا ٱلْقُرْبَىٰ حَقَّهُۥ وَٱلْمِسْكِينَ وَٱبْنَ ٱلسَّبِيلِ وَلَا تُبَذِّرْ تَبْذِيرًا ۝٢٦ إِنَّ ٱلْمُبَذِّرِينَ كَانُوٓا۟ إِخْوَٰنَ ٱلشَّيَٰطِينِ ۖ وَكَانَ ٱلشَّيْطَٰنُ لِرَبِّهِۦ كَفُورًا ۝٢٧

٢٨٤

عَسَىٰ رَبُّكُمْ أَن يَرْحَمَكُمْ ۚ وَإِنْ عُدتُّمْ عُدْنَا ۘ وَجَعَلْنَا جَهَنَّمَ لِلْكَافِرِينَ حَصِيرًا ۝٨ إِنَّ هَٰذَا الْقُرْءَانَ يَهْدِى لِلَّتِى هِىَ أَقْوَمُ وَيُبَشِّرُ الْمُؤْمِنِينَ الَّذِينَ يَعْمَلُونَ الصَّٰلِحَٰتِ أَنَّ لَهُمْ أَجْرًا كَبِيرًا ۝٩ وَأَنَّ الَّذِينَ لَا يُؤْمِنُونَ بِالْءَاخِرَةِ أَعْتَدْنَا لَهُمْ عَذَابًا أَلِيمًا ۝١٠ وَيَدْعُ الْإِنسَٰنُ بِالشَّرِّ دُعَاءَهُۥ بِالْخَيْرِ ۖ وَكَانَ الْإِنسَٰنُ عَجُولًا ۝١١ وَجَعَلْنَا الَّيْلَ وَالنَّهَارَ ءَايَتَيْنِ ۖ فَمَحَوْنَا ءَايَةَ الَّيْلِ وَجَعَلْنَا ءَايَةَ النَّهَارِ مُبْصِرَةً لِّتَبْتَغُوا۟ فَضْلًا مِّن رَّبِّكُمْ وَلِتَعْلَمُوا۟ عَدَدَ السِّنِينَ وَالْحِسَابَ ۚ وَكُلَّ شَىْءٍ فَصَّلْنَٰهُ تَفْصِيلًا ۝١٢ وَكُلَّ إِنسَٰنٍ أَلْزَمْنَٰهُ طَٰٓئِرَهُۥ فِى عُنُقِهِۦ ۖ وَنُخْرِجُ لَهُۥ يَوْمَ الْقِيَٰمَةِ كِتَٰبًا يَلْقَىٰهُ مَنشُورًا ۝١٣ اقْرَأْ كِتَٰبَكَ كَفَىٰ بِنَفْسِكَ الْيَوْمَ عَلَيْكَ حَسِيبًا ۝١٤ مَّنِ اهْتَدَىٰ فَإِنَّمَا يَهْتَدِى لِنَفْسِهِۦ ۖ وَمَن ضَلَّ فَإِنَّمَا يَضِلُّ عَلَيْهَا ۚ وَلَا تَزِرُ وَازِرَةٌ وِزْرَ أُخْرَىٰ ۗ وَمَا كُنَّا مُعَذِّبِينَ حَتَّىٰ نَبْعَثَ رَسُولًا ۝١٥ وَإِذَا أَرَدْنَا أَن نُّهْلِكَ قَرْيَةً أَمَرْنَا مُتْرَفِيهَا فَفَسَقُوا۟ فِيهَا فَحَقَّ عَلَيْهَا الْقَوْلُ فَدَمَّرْنَٰهَا تَدْمِيرًا ۝١٦ وَكَمْ أَهْلَكْنَا مِنَ الْقُرُونِ مِنۢ بَعْدِ نُوحٍ ۗ وَكَفَىٰ بِرَبِّكَ بِذُنُوبِ عِبَادِهِۦ خَبِيرًۢا بَصِيرًا ۝١٧

سورة الإسراء

بِسْمِ اللَّهِ الرَّحْمَٰنِ الرَّحِيمِ

سُبْحَانَ الَّذِي أَسْرَىٰ بِعَبْدِهِ لَيْلًا مِّنَ الْمَسْجِدِ الْحَرَامِ إِلَى الْمَسْجِدِ الْأَقْصَى الَّذِي بَارَكْنَا حَوْلَهُ لِنُرِيَهُ مِنْ آيَاتِنَا إِنَّهُ هُوَ السَّمِيعُ الْبَصِيرُ ۝ وَآتَيْنَا مُوسَى الْكِتَابَ وَجَعَلْنَاهُ هُدًى لِّبَنِي إِسْرَائِيلَ أَلَّا تَتَّخِذُوا مِن دُونِي وَكِيلًا ۝ ذُرِّيَّةَ مَنْ حَمَلْنَا مَعَ نُوحٍ إِنَّهُ كَانَ عَبْدًا شَكُورًا ۝ وَقَضَيْنَا إِلَىٰ بَنِي إِسْرَائِيلَ فِي الْكِتَابِ لَتُفْسِدُنَّ فِي الْأَرْضِ مَرَّتَيْنِ وَلَتَعْلُنَّ عُلُوًّا كَبِيرًا ۝ فَإِذَا جَاءَ وَعْدُ أُولَاهُمَا بَعَثْنَا عَلَيْكُمْ عِبَادًا لَّنَا أُولِي بَأْسٍ شَدِيدٍ فَجَاسُوا خِلَالَ الدِّيَارِ وَكَانَ وَعْدًا مَّفْعُولًا ۝ ثُمَّ رَدَدْنَا لَكُمُ الْكَرَّةَ عَلَيْهِمْ وَأَمْدَدْنَاكُم بِأَمْوَالٍ وَبَنِينَ وَجَعَلْنَاكُمْ أَكْثَرَ نَفِيرًا ۝ إِنْ أَحْسَنتُمْ أَحْسَنتُمْ لِأَنفُسِكُمْ وَإِنْ أَسَأْتُمْ فَلَهَا فَإِذَا جَاءَ وَعْدُ الْآخِرَةِ لِيَسُوءُوا وُجُوهَكُمْ وَلِيَدْخُلُوا الْمَسْجِدَ كَمَا دَخَلُوهُ أَوَّلَ مَرَّةٍ وَلِيُتَبِّرُوا مَا عَلَوْا تَتْبِيرًا ۝

Printed in Great Britain
by Amazon